9/03

The Company Image

Building Your Identity and
Influence in the Marketplace

Elinor Selame
Joe Selame

Selame Design

with *the editorial collaboration*
of F. Peter Model

WILEY

John Wiley & Sons
New York   Chichester   Brisbane   Toronto   Singapore

Library of Congress Cataloging-in-Publication Data:
Selame, Elinor.
    The company image: building your identity and influence in the
marketplace / Elinor Selame, Joseph Selame (Selame Design), with the
editorial collaboration of F. Peter Model.
      p. cm.
    ISBN 0-471-62424-1
    1. Corporate image.   2. Industrial design coordination.
I. Selame, Joe.   II. Model, F. Peter.   III. Selame Design (Firm)
IV. Title.
HD59.2.S44 1988   87-34924
659.2′85—dc 19   CIP

Printed in the United States of America
10 9 8 7 6 5 4 3 2 1

In Memoriam

In 1986 we were personally and professionally touched by the deaths of three pioneers in the design world. The passing of Raymond F. Loewy, 92, Walter P. Margulies, 73, and George Nelson, 78, ended an era in the history of design.

Their lives touched our daily work, and their deaths inspired us to communicate their convictions, along with our own, to the business community through this book. We believe each of these men left a unique legacy through their individual and collective works.

To Raymond Loewy, style was a part of function. Envisioning a sleek, aerodynamic future for American industry, Loewy invented industrial design as a profession. His industrial designs for Sears Roebuck and Company's Coldspot Refrigerator in 1935, the S-1 locomotive, the Avanti, and the 1953 Studebaker Starliner exemplify the "Loewy look."

His design prowess spread to packaging, graphics, and corporate identity, with his designs for the Coca-Cola bottle, the Lucky Strike cigarette package, and corporate identities for Exxon, Shell, the U.S. Postal Service, and countless others.

Walter Margulies made corporate identity a business by entering boardrooms across America from American Express, Bendix, and Chrysler to United Technologies, Weyerhaeuser, and Xerox. Margulies brought attention to the bottom-line implications of corporate identity and demonstrated how unified visual marketing themes can reshape a corporation's image among its key publics and distinguish it from the competition.

George Nelson proved that successful companies use good product design as one of their marketing strategies. His home and office furniture designs for Herman Miller are world-renowned classics. In addition, Nelson introduced designers Charles Eames and Isamu Noguchi to Herman Miller, enabling the firm to become a leader and innovator in the furniture industry. Nelson's belief that design is central to all aspects of everyday life led to the development of the pedestrian mall—or, "grass on Main Street."

Whether on Main Street or Wall Street, the designs of Loewy, Margulies, and Nelson changed the way we live and work. They elevated design to a highly respected profession, and convinced corporate America of the business value of good design. Their contributions opened opportunities for the next generation of designers. As their honored heirs, we challenge ourselves and our corporate clients to take responsibility for good design. It improves the quality of life, and it's good business.

Elinor and Joe Selame, IDSA

Preface

Assuming a new corporate identity, like donning a custom-tailored ensemble for the first time, is at once a commitment to the present and an investment in the future.

Carefully selected and cut from a variety of materials, individually styled and tastefully executed, and made to last, corporate identity (CI), like a good suit, allows business to exude the confidence it needs to win friends and influence people. Dale Carnegie was not wrong.

Whether one spends millions or only thousands of dollars on a corporate identity program, the expenditure is no longer undertaken solely to allow the enterprise to stand above, and apart from, the crowd. These days, CI also serves as a long-term strategic weapon in the battle for multinational market share.

Corporate identity gives every business the ability to determine for itself the kind of face—or "image"—it wants to project to its various publics, both inside and outside the organization, at home and abroad.

The fact that so many corporations now attach such enormous importance to their appearance only reaffirms that in the waning years of the 20th century (to paraphrase a 17th-century poet) "No business is an island, entire of itself."

In recent years, the public has begun taking a far greater interest in the booming business of shaping such images.

Creating corporate identity is a profession that has grown exponentially in direct proportion to the number of companies that have undergone mergers, acquisitions, leveraged buy-outs, and similar transformations.

What used to be covered sporadically only by trade journals is now becoming legitimate grist for the news media mill. Lately identity changes at major corporations rate front page notice.

As professional identity consultants for nearly 30 years, we view this as a healthy development.

The public *should* be privy to the process whereby old names, which no longer describe the nature of the business or do not reflect current operating realities, are replaced by new names. Tired symbols are phased out and replaced by visual abstracts that will strike many as meaningless at first, but which, ultimately, are accepted if not always fully understood.

But what astonishes us, even after nearly three decades of serving businesses large and small, is how little corporate management understands that process; how many business leaders still regard corporate identity molding as an unaffordable luxury or frill rather than as an inescapable expense of doing business properly; and how often even those who do appreciate its value decline to become personally involved in effecting visual change.

It is not a matter of doubting CI's value, they will point out, but that they simply do not have the time to immerse themselves in so time-consuming a process, one to which, they solemnly maintain, they have so little to contribute.

They are wrong. Leaders in corporate management have a lot to contribute. What they fail to understand is that CI is much more than selecting a new name and symbol, or improving an old one, and integrally more than glossy corporate cosmetics.

CI, properly planned and systematized, is the visual expression of the corporation as it sees itself and as it wishes to be viewed by others. It is the banner under which it goes to market 365 days a year. And not always just to sell goods and services but also to explain itself to a number of publics—customers, vendors, employees, investors, legislators, financial analysts, and others.

As such, ensuring that this visual expression remains clear, consistent, and effective is possibly the single most important—and *lasting*—decision any CEO will make during his or her term in office.

"Paying attention to your visual marketing strategy and making your company a forerunner in its industry," Marvin Traub told us, "is worth all the time in the world."

Mr. Traub is chairman of Bloomingdale's, whose brilliant (and profitable) use of image marketing has made it the most-imitated mass retail operation in the world. Even the managers of Moscow's GUM stores have traveled to Manhattan to observe and learn firsthand.

Twelve years ago, in *Developing a Corporate Identity: How To Stand Out in the Crowd* (New York: Lebhar-Friedman) we produced the definitive textbook on CI. It went through four printings and found a responsive audience.

That book is now out of print. The business world has grown and changed considerably since its original publication, most notably in the degree to which corporate accountability has taken on a life of its own.

Increasingly top management now recognizes that names and symbols can no longer be regarded as "corporate window dressing," and that a singular clarity of purpose and a sales-generating CI rarely emerge from consensus decision-making. One can search the world for statues and never find one that pays homage to a committee.

Clearly, selecting the right name and symbol is too important a decision to be left entirely to chance. Or to a computer.

The belief that the CI process must begin and end in the front office is one we have repeatedly addressed over the years at client meetings, in numerous magazine articles, speeches, and seminars. We do so again in *The Company Image: Building Your Identity and Influence in the Marketplace.*

Is such a book necessary? We think so. There seems to be no shortage of books that depict such well-recognized CI programs as those of IBM, Olivetti, Mobil, AT&T, CBS, and Chrysler. They make for exciting reading, paying homage as they do both to the skills of many celebrated corporate design consultants and to the elevated tastes of their clients.

What they do *not* do is address such questions as: Why was change called for? What did it ultimately cost? Where did the project start? Who was in charge? Why was it necessary to hire outsiders? How did these companies benefit?

We, too, were curious, so we went back to some of the key people involved and asked them. Often, the answers we got were surprisingly candid, raising issues that had never occurred to us as professionals. Over a period of years, as we listened to the tapes, this book began to take shape.

Since today's time-conscious CEOs and their key executives find themselves inundated with all sorts of nuts-and-bolts literature, we did not think any purpose would be served in producing yet another "how-to" casebook that might be bucked down the line to a middle manager along with a note from the executive secretary, "The boss wants you to read this."

We wanted to do a book the boss himself would take home to read.

Which is why we tackled the subject in a style familiar to busy executives: as a work of people-dominated business journalism—not just what-where-and-how but also who-when-and-why.

To do so, we relied extensively on many hours of taped interviews and correspondence, and rounded out the transcripts by tapping numerous data bases and clipping services.

We are indebted, especially, to our past and present clients, who spoke freely of their initial doubts as well as of their obvious satisfaction with the programs they commissioned.

A special thanks to our partner and managing director, Greg Kolligian, whose considerable marketing and management skills helped guide many of these programs to their successful conclusion.

We are equally appreciative of the number of participating CEOs and their aides; although not clients of Selame Design they nonetheless thought well enough of our project to give generously of their time and to provide access to their files and archives.

Newton Lower Falls, Massachusetts
June 1988

Elinor Selame
Joseph Selame

Contents

The parameters of corporate identity

Harry W. O'Neill likes to tell the famous Mark Twain story about the missionary addressing the cannibals.

"They listened with the greatest interest to everything he had to say . . . and *then* . . . they ate *him*."

Mister O'Neill is former vice chairman of Opinion Research Corporation (ORC), the Princeton-based polling arm of Arthur D. Little, Inc.

O'Neill says he's in "the corporate image business." Every other year, ORC researchers conduct a "Corporate Reputation Study" for which some *Fortune* 500 companies pay as much as $50,000—just to learn what the American public thinks of them.

Apparently, not very much. The latest (Summer 1987) ORC study shows that Americans hold Big Business in fairly low esteem.

- 8 of 10 Americans feel that as companies get bigger, their customer relationships grow colder and more impersonal.
- 79 percent fear that in just about every industrial category the consumer is at the mercy of one or two "dominant" companies.
- 6 out of 10 believe business people would do anything to make a buck, preferably at the consumer's expense. More than 50 percent believe profits are out of line, that business makes 34 cents on the dollar (when, in fact, government data peg it closer to four cents).

"We find," says O'Neill, "that large companies inspire the trust and confidence of very *few* people." Only 13 percent are willing to give business a high approval rating in the areas of ethics and morality.[1]

John C. Whitehead, erstwhile CEO of the investment firm of Goldman, Sachs & Co., points out that "What sets apart the company selling at 16 times earnings from the company selling at six times earnings is investor perception: what's management like? What sort of record do they have? Are its products any good? Plus lots of intangible factors that add up to a gut feeling that the outfit's OK."[2]

William (Mil) Batten, an ex-President of the New York Stock Exchange who, in his earlier post as J.C. Penney board chairman presided over the transformation of that venerable chain into an up-to-date international retailer, agrees that these days the sizzle may be as important as the steak.

"It's not enough just to *change* what you are. The customers must *perceive* that you've changed."

---

[1]Personal interview of Harry O'Neill by F. Peter Model. In January 1988, Harry W. O'Neill, Vice Chairman, joined the Roper Organization.
[2]John C. Whitehead, *Design Sense*, Lippincott & Margulies.

Batten reveals that many regular Penney customers, in mall-intercept studies after the company had spent millions on store renovation and label systemizing in implementing their new identity, barely commented on the new decor. Instead, Batten recalls, "They said they were impressed by the improvement in *the quality of our merchandise.*" Yet, the one thing Penney's hadn't tinkered with was the quality of its merchandise: it didn't have to. That had not been Penney's problem.

"All that was changed," Batten adds, "was our presentation, our image."[3]

Most people do not differentiate between "image" and "identity." Though these terms are like apples and oranges, they are seen as growing on the same tree.

The reason is simple: images tend to be gradually perceived, while identities are quickly observed. Moreover, images are *evolutionary* and tend to be made up of small, often unrelated parts. Identities can be created on a drawing board and, like mosaics, carefully and deliberately pieced together and—more importantly—*controlled.* In corporate identity, it's not only what you say, but often the visual way in which you say it. It may not be the corporate or brand name that's the problem; it could be the typestyle used. Words and initials take on different meanings depending on how they're visualized. (See Figure 1.1.)

Again, citing the ORC study, we learn that seven Americans in 10 (71 percent) feel that a company's reputation depends more on what the company itself does than on events outside the company and beyond its control. "If a company suffers from a poor image," says O'Neill, "it has only itself to blame."

This is not to say a poor image can be cleaned up by bringing in a corporate identity consultant. Hiring a consultant unquestionably would be a major step, but may not be the place to start.

The message is getting through: business *wants* to be perceived as being "user-friendly." It is spending considerable sums probing, fretting over, and *doing* something constructive about improving its public image. PR and corporate advertising budgets are up, and so is spending for corporate and product identity.

Doing especially well these days are the name merchants—a new breed of consultants whose computers can spew out more names than are in the Manhattan telephone book. In 1986, they helped change the names of 1,382 companies and institutions—an increase of 33 percent over the year before.

ORC's research, based on lengthy interviews with a random, scientifically selected nationwide sample of more than 1,000 adults, shows these efforts may be starting to pay off where it matters most: in consumer *perceptions.*

Two thirds of the public (68 percent) says that "In most cases, the more they know about a company, the more favorable they feel towards it. And almost nine out of 10 shoppers (87 percent) say that when they can choose between products

---

[3]Personal interview of William (Mil) Batten by author.

STINK

In this example, notice how a word takes on a different meaning by simply changing a type style. One could be a perfumed aroma, the other something else again.

FRIEND   friend

This example shows how upper and lower primer type looks more believable than caps in Gothic. The caps one yells insincerely that it is a friend, whereas the lower case Roman states its case simply and quietly.

Like the volume adjustment on your radio, type can project a message softly, or it can shout. A sensitive use of type can make the difference between a softly persuasive message or a rude, loud demand.

1.1 *Talking Type*
Gothic capital letters evoke urgency, power, authority. News headlines would be less frightening or effective in a lightface Roman. On the other hand, a note to a friend would look like a threat if rendered in Franklin Gothic.

and services that are similar in quality and price, *the reputation of the company will often determine which product or service is bought."*

Innumerable studies and reports have shown that over 80 percent of what we learn is through *sight.* In like manner a company's visual presentation must play a crucial role in projecting its reputation.

Recognition of what planned corporate identity can do comes at a time when American business is in great flux. Deregulation of such industries as banking, transportation, and telecommunications has opened the floodgates to corporate restructuring and repositioning.

"Old" conglomerates are now stripping themselves of subsidiaries that no longer fit today's marketing modes. A case-in-point: Gulf + Western Industries, which, having spun off or sold off all of its "heavy" industries, is now mainly in leisure-time activities and financial services. Though retaining its well known G+W logo, it now calls itself just plain Gulf + Western Incorporated.

For every hydra-headed conglomerate being restructured into monoglomerates, such as food-oriented Beatrice, there are estimated to be three overweight goliaths going the other way, "downsizing" themselves to become leaner and meaner competitors in new areas. Thus, to signal the reduced importance of steel in its marketing mix, U.S. Steel became USX.

A 1986 survey by the Association of National Advertisers of 362 of the country's major corporations shows 44 percent of them putting "building corporate awareness" at the very top of their agendas.

As these corporations juggle their priorities, new visual identities assume an importance they never had. Says Joel Portugal, a principal in the design firm that produces an annual tally of corporate name changes, "They have become manageable assets, tools that are used to help get them where they want to go."[4]

If nothing else, new names provide the contextual framework in which to place the transformation process. To stick with the old while everything else changes is to risk being perceived by a critical public as diluting rather than enhancing corporate equity.

The change need not be flamboyant. Change may be best made quietly and tastefully. There are many subtle ways of altering perceptions.

Consider the change that has overcome Black & Decker, the erstwhile supplier of home power tools. After it acquired the General Electric Small Appliance division, B&D changed its entire marketing approach, while fine-tuning its new corporate identity. It now sells to the wife of the man who buys the power tools.

An even more startling transformation may be that which is taking place in the old Sears, Roebuck Company. The catalog is still here, but the outhouse image

---

[4]Personal interview of Joel Portugal by author.

has followed the long-forgotten Alvah Roebuck to limbo. Now it's just plain Sears—and what brings in most of the profits are the services of Allstate (insurance), Dean Witter (investments), and Coldwell Banker (real estate).

Nowhere is identity change more prevalent these days than in the financial services area. Take the nation's banks, traditionally bastions of the *status quo*. It used to be an article of faith that all banks were "First," "National," or "Amalgamated." Now that they are going *interstate* (and causing all sorts of identity crises for the old local banks whose turfs are being trespassed and trod upon) banks are sporting all sorts of unbank-like identities.

Utilities, newly imbued with the spirit of *laissez-faire*, are now dabbling in all sorts of interesting new market-driven profit centers, and are sparing little expense to appear far less haughty and more accessible to the consumer. Who would have thought that AT&T's forced divestiture of its 22 telephone companies would lead it to take on the friendly, neighborhood home electronics store? Mickey Mouse telephones by AT&T, indeed!

All this corporate restructuring has an impact on a very wide front, especially in such image-shaping industries as advertising, public relations, and corporate identity. At the March 1987 annual meeting of the American Association of Advertising Agencies in Boca Raton, incoming AAAA chairperson Charlotte Beers ominously warned her peers that they, too, might find themselves restructured into irrelevancy.

"Clients ask themselves, 'Couldn't we do the same or maybe a better marketing job for less money by exploring alternatives to media advertising?'" She did not have to identify these "alternatives," or the nature of the consultants who would be hired to implement them. Corporate identity (CI) is not normally seen as an advertising agency service.

Image vs. identity defined

"No facelifting can put a gloss on a faulty image," observes Rawleigh Warner Jr., the urbane, Princeton-educated former board chairman of Mobil Corporation, whose $20 million CI overhaul two decades ago had enormous impact on its global perception.

"At best, it can only reflect the company's true character."[5]

_____

[5] Personal interview of Rawleigh Warner Jr. by author.

Most business people, regardless of the size of their companies, understand "image" to be one of those intangibles Goldman, Sachs' John Whitehead talks about—*impressions* that are shaped and reshaped to produce the most favorable public perception. They think most of the image-bending is achieved through favorable treatment by the media.

We wish it were that easy.

Perhaps the word image ought to be embargoed until it's better understood—not for what is is, but for what it isn't.

Howard Luck Gossage, a San Francisco adman whose campaigns for QANTAS Airways, Paul Masson Vineyards, and Eagle Shirtmakers are still being talked about 17 years after his death, *despised* the word "image." He condemned its use as a grammatical aberration—insisting that "Identity is what one really *is,* while Image only means how one appears to other people."

Gossage also felt that "Image has a somewhat fraudulent sound, as though you are trying to put something over."

Actually, the reason he preferred *Identity* over *Image* is that Identity requires much less upkeep.

"Identity is like the sun. It radiates energy from a solid mass. Image, on the other hand, is like a balloon: it is all surface and spends too much time avoiding pin pricks."[6]

American business spends an inordinate amount of time and money trying to avoid those pin pricks. And it knows that in an age of visual communications—where attention spans are measured in seconds, not minutes—verbal communication can no longer do the job as effectively as graphic shorthand.

Like it or not, every commercial enterprise has a visual identity. It may be conveyed by logotype, annual report, letterhead, truck signage, advertising, packaging, architecture, and landscaping. More likely, an enterprise's identity lies in the *totality* of its appearance, and one rotten apple can spoil the visual barrel.

That so many companies still don't appreciate the role good design can play in shaping attitudes remains a puzzle.

Looks may not be everything, but when intelligently applied, they can have a powerful subliminal effect.

"Like the missionary appearing before the cannibals," Harry O'Neill believes, "today's chief executive may *think* he is well-tuned in to the world around him through his PR people or his Old Boy Network, but he really isn't. The media, on which so many still depend to do their bidding, can be dangerously two-edged."

---

[6]Howard Luck Gossage, speech to Western States Advertising Agencies Assn., Los Angeles, excerpted in *Advertising Age,* May 5, 1969.

Appearances count

In the primitive days of the public relations profession—back when PR pioneer Ivy Lee tried to "humanize" John D. Rockefeller Sr. by persuading him to pass out dimes to newsboys—Sigmund Freud's nephew, Edward L. Bernays, coined the expression, "the engineering of the public consent."

Bernays, now in his nineties, is still counseling management. "No business today can function without the public's consent," he reiterates, "but winning that consent seems to be tougher today than at any time I can recall."[7]

His recall is excellent, and it goes back to such Bernays clients as A. P. Giannini, founder of Bank of America, Alfred P. Sloan of General Motors—not to mention Henry Ford, David Sarnoff, Henry Luce, and others who placed a premium on corporate identity.

"Nothing has changed," says Bernays. "Appearance still matters a great deal."

Identity: deeper than a symbol

The only advantage today's business person has over the hapless missionary in Harry O'Neill's story is that "today's cannibals no longer kill and eat, they just walk away and ignore you."

On a practical, street-level basis, that is no advantage at all. In fact, being eaten may be preferable. In an April 1987 interview with *Advertising Age* about how Mobil Corp. hoped to resuscitate its ailing Montgomery Ward & Co. retail subsidiary—the antithesis to Sears—so that it could be sold or spun off, CEO Bernard Brennan spoke about image and identity. "Our biggest problem is that people just don't dislike us. In many cases, they just *ignore* us."

Yet too many companies still treat identity as something that can be whipped up after hours by an in-house art department. Not appreciating the direct correlation between a one-time investment and dividends that seem to flow forever, they take the "money-saving" approach of finding a suitable graphic gimmick.

Edwin I. Colodny was senior marketing executive at Allegheny Airlines in 1974 when the company began thinking of becoming a major carrier. Now board chairman and CEO of USAir Group Inc., as the airline is now known, Colodny says, "Corporate identity is more than a new letterhead, a Band-Aid solution.

---

[7]Personal interview of Edward L. Bernays by F. Peter Model.

"It must be applied across-the-board as it must accurately reflect that company's business, its operating philosophy, its corporate culture. An identity cannot be forged overnight in some ad agency's back room."[8]

Many advertising people recognize the importance of corporate identity in the "marketing mix," even if they do not always appreciate the role of the CI practitioner in helping to shape overall long-term corporate strategies.

The turf-protective attitude will quite likely change as more mega-corporations emerge and feel the need to impart an aura of parental responsibility.

Robert C. Plumb, manager of GE's business-to-business communications, spends $20 million a year on advertising "to the trade"—less than half of the $45 million GE's consumer divisions allocate to their advertising programs. He is one of those advertisers Charlotte Beers warned the 4A's about, because Plumb would like to see more money spent on noncommissionable corporate ID.[9]

Plumb explains, "You're talking to people who don't want to know every last detail of a product's features. They want to know what 'it's going to do for me'—in plain, simple language." The GE logo does that very well. So do the initials IBM. In office equipment circles, there's a saying, "No purchasing agent ever got fired for specifying IBM."

It's not just a matter of Confucian logic, of a picture being worth a thousand words. It's that there's just so much advertising that the human mind can absorb.

The average American consumer is exposed to over 560 advertisements a day, of which—media researchers sheepishly admit—only 76 are "noticed," and only 12 "remembered." We are so inured to the surfeit of commercialism that we instinctively screen out all but the most memorable messages.

The viewer watching TV six hours a day is "exposed" to approximately 90 commercials of varying length. Despite the fact that we learn mostly by sight, saturation advertising seems to have a negative effect: the more commercials we see at one sitting, the fewer we will remember.

More specifically, in a sequence of five back-to-back commercials, our attention is likely to peak after the first 30 or 60 seconds, thereafter dropping sharply to the point where the fifth commercial becomes a blur.

The cost of trying to breach this mental barrier is staggering: in 1986, U.S. business spent almost $27 billion in newspaper advertising, $22 billion on television, and $5 billion in magazines. But is anybody looking?

In January 1987, just before the telecast of Super Bowl XXI—when a single, 60-second commercial sold for $1.2 million—New York's Director of Water

---

[8]Personal interview of Edwin I. Colodny by author.
[9]"Creativity Moves In," *Industry Week*, January 26, 1987.

Resources pleaded that viewers not all rush to the bathroom at once, lest water pressure drop to a level where fire hydrants would become useless.

Put another way, $20,000 a second was flushed down the drain. Is it any wonder that business needs all the help it can get?

Stretching the ad budget

Use of a strong corporate symbol in the visual context of the TV advertisement may not return water pressure to prehalftime levels, but when intelligently applied to all other forms of advertising, it will almost certainly stretch the consumer's attention span, to say nothing of the overall ad budget.

At a time when more corporations take to TV to explain their positions to shareholders and legislators—notably Sunday mornings on the three major commercial networks and throughout the week on PBS—the corporate symbol in advertising is becoming a "given."

Perception Research Services Inc., a New Jersey-based testing firm that tracks advertising/package design effectiveness through consumer eye response, finds that on the average, 15 percent fewer people see the advertiser's name in corporate print ads than in all other ads. That's because many corporate ads lack a clearcut corporate identity. Here's an example:

In 1985, the nation's fourth-largest property and life insurer—the Travelers—was found to be suffering from overall awareness problems. Like all the other major underwriters, Travelers was expanding its folio of consumer services with home mortgages, pension planning, HMOs, and other instruments. Compared to Prudential's Rock, and John Hancock's signature, and even to Metropolitan's Snoopy, Lucy, and Charlie Brown, however, Travelers lacked instantaneous recognition.

But, according to William Esty Co. advertising account supervisor Patricia Stewart, the research did show that its historic umbrella symbol was "a highly recognizable mnemonic device."[10] That is to say, it jogged the memory.

The resulting $2.5 million ad campaign built entirely around (or under) the Travelers' red umbrella, virtually turned consumer perceptions 360 degrees: in test after test against rival insurer ads, respondents were "more predisposed" to hearing from the Travelers than from the others.

We will be returning to the subject of advertising and corporate ID throughout the book. For the moment, it may suffice to recognize the growing importance of visual identity in today's total marketing strategy.

---

[10]"The Travelers Gains New Awareness with Old Symbol," *Inside Print*, January 1987.

From time to time, articles appear in the business press about advertising campaigns that failed, for one reason or another—the wrong copy or art approach, inappropriate or insufficient media exposure, and so forth.

During the 27-odd years, however, that we have practiced our profession as designers and visual *marketing* consultants—conceptualizing, developing, and then sustaining corporate identities through all kinds of social and business cycles—we have never read or heard of a business that failed to profit from wanting to look better, smarter, and worldlier.

2

The options for
changing identity

In today's fluid business environment, when hardly a week goes by without another friendly (or hostile) takeover, merger, acquisition, or spin-off, it's becoming increasingly difficult to keep track of the players.

Moreover, as the line-up changes, so do the rules of the game.

"I find I'm wasting time these days deciphering acronyms," complains New York investment banker Pierre L. Schoenheimer, scanning the desktop terminal of his on-line computer. "Maybe they should pass a law that if a company chooses initials over a name it has *got* to be the trading symbol."[1]

As more and more companies opt to shed once memorable names to assume "vanilla" identities or deliberately meaningless acronyms that are also hard to pronounce, not only traders but the general public are getting testy (and nervous). We've heard of situations where in the midst of the change, employees begin to experience their own identity crisis.

It is a crisis that, sooner or later, is faced by every organization, whether in the private or public sector, whether it deals in products or services.

"Like it or not," observes British industrial designer Wolff Olins, "their identity exists. The question that management must answer is whether *they* control that identity or whether that identity controls *them.*"[2]

Just what do we mean when we speak of *corporate identity?*

Identity isn't just a symbol or signature that appears on the letterhead, a trademark or service mark that is used on packaging and advertising, or the decals on the company-leased fleet of trucks. Nor is it just plant architecture or office interiors, the company flag fluttering below the Stars & Stripes, or the signage that points the way to headquarters.

It is all of these, the totality of split-second perceptions that the human eye takes in. And it is more: the appearance of the package, or the advertising supporting that package's introduction; the dividend checks, and the annual report; the interoffice memos and the billing statements.

It can be accidental, unplanned, and therefore chaotic; or it can be purposeful, planned, and structured—the way a corporation wants to be seen by its various constituents: customers, shareholders, analysts, bankers, suppliers, the press, employees, and plant communities.

---

[1]Even that may not work. Former Booz-Allen management consultant Henry E. Figgie Jr. bought the venerable Automatic Sprinkler System of Ohio of Youngstown, Ohio, and turned it into a $1 billion conglomerate with 37 divisions. He then went public. As it was imperative to shuck the fire-control image, the company was renamed A-T-O after its trading symbol. Wall Streeters still could not figure out what A-T-O was, or did. Depending on how the market behaved, it was known as either "A Terrific Organization" or "Associated Turkeys of Ohio." Fed up, but over the chairman's protest, the board in desperation took the PR firm's recommendation and in 1981 renamed it "Figgie International Corp." Now analysts want to know, "What's a Figgie?"

[2]Wolff Olins, *Wolff Olins' Guide to Corporate Identity.*

When does a company need to organize its corporate identity? Ideally, as well as practically, from the very first moment it opens its doors for business.

In the beginning, of course, design implementation is fairly easy to handle: the chosen identity is applied consistently on every piece of visual communication the company plans to use—letterhead, checks, office forms, advertising, publicity releases, factory or showroom signs, etc.

As long as the entire operation remains concentrated and cohesive, consistency is pretty much assured. But as the organization expands physically and its communications needs multiply, the first thing to go is apt to be consistency. With more than one cook in charge of the kettle, coordination and control of corporate graphics gain the kind of importance few may have foreseen the day the business got started.

Most entrepreneurs have neither the time nor the patience to take proper charge of corporate identity. Rather quickly, the "system" starts falling apart as various identities begin to appear, designed piecemeal by various outside suppliers or staff personnel who use existing supplies as their standards. At first, there is visual confusion, nothing dramatically different but still not quite up to the first run. There is still time for someone to take notice and to restore order.

It is only after years of indifference verging on neglect that visual chaos presents itself. By then, it may be too late to order a simple fall-back position. For as growing companies merge with and acquire other companies, develop and expand new product lines, visual cohesiveness disintegrates—and the impact may be felt clear to the top of the organization.

Ron Kareken, Director of *Eastman Kodak's* Trademark Legal Staff, recalls how, in 1971, management began dealing with this very problem.

"We had been growing rapidly during the past 15 years, both through acquiring other companies and introducing new products and consumer services. All of these activities confronted the legal department with new names and trademarks, as well as a variety of package designs.

"When we stepped back to take a conscious look at our worldwide marketing identity, we realized that despite our singular name, we had many varied and unrelated identities. This was bound to confuse not just our dealers but also our customers. It was then we decided to develop a more coordinated visual identity system."[3] (See Figure 2.1.)

Kodak's discovery and experience are hardly unique. In all probability, Kodak's problems, and the way it went about solving them, were not much different from those of other multidivisional and/or global companies.

---

[3]Personal interview of Ron Kareken by author.

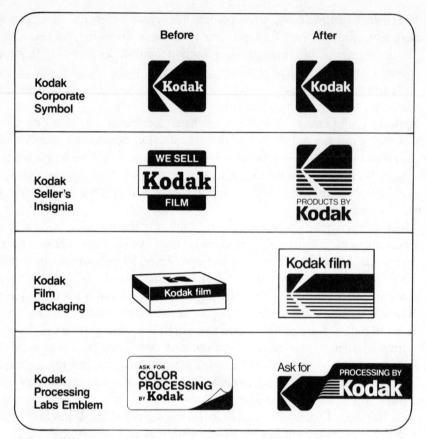

2.1 *Kodak*
Building on the existing Kodak corporate mark with an updated typeface, a multi-product and services identity was developed to:

- provide a consistent international trade identity
- reinforce Kodak's reputation as a progressive and innovative company
- achieve immediate and lasting recognition among consumers
- simplify language translation

These new designs use the familiar yellow colors and the Kodak name. In addition, they are designed to simplify and unify Kodak trade identity on a worldwide basis.

Customers who see one of these marks will know that they have found a source of Kodak products or services, or a business that uses them in preparing its own product or service.

Design Credit: Selame Design

Multi-divisional options

This is not to say that there is only one way to treat a corporate "identity crisis" or that finding the correct identity becomes a matter of working down a standardized list of options and selecting the one that seems suitable.

For what appears, at first, to be a logical solution may turn out to be anything but logical once exploratory discussions between client and consultant end and the actual research and design process begins. Nor is finding the right identity a matter of divine inspiration; what oftens appears to be artfully simple design, may, in fact, be the end product of some deep and painfully protracted group thinking.

For our purposes, however, let us narrow down the options and examine the three most popular categories of corporate identity:

1. Monolithic

Here the organization uses one name, symbol/typestyle in virtually every application that comes to mind, right down to matchbook covers in the executive dining room. In monolithic CI, whatever identities may be projected by the divisions, subsidiaries, support groups, advertisements, and literature, all serve the single purpose of reinforcing at all times the identity of the parent. Examples: IBM Corp., CBS Inc., AT&T.

2. Endorsement

There is more than one design approach possible to link the parent with the offspring. Examples:

A. *Adopting* a unilateral mark and signature style for holding companies, divisions, and subsidiaries that, in turn, retain individual names within a carefully structured design discipline (e.g., Eastern Gas & Fuel). (See Figure 2.2.)
B. *Positioning* the individual divisions with equity in their own names, either with a primary or secondary position to the parent's CI. Who has top billing depends on the corporation's strategic and marketing objectives, Shearson-Lehman Brothers/American Express. (See Figure 2.3.)
C. *Retaining* the acquired subsidiary or division's name when the unit is a leader in its own field, e.g., General Motors' Hughes Aircraft, Philip Morris' Miller Brewing. No purpose would be served sublimating the identity of an acquired unit into the parental CI, least of all when two well-established packaged goods giants come together; for example, Philip Morris' acquisition of General Foods.

Eastern Gas and Fuel Associates

2.2 *Eastern G & F Associates*
Eastern's identity system incorporates as many of the existing divisions' identities as possible, to provide continuity. The new symbol preserves the circle that was so prominent in many of their old company marks; incorporated into it is an abstract impression of energy. The basic lettering style for all divisions was built on the existing Boston Gas logo. The unifying mark and type style identify the various divisions as part of the total organization.

Design Credit: Selame Design

2.3 *American Express*
Design credit (American Express symbol): Lippincott & Margulies

3. Corporate or branded

Where both identities are utilized at the same time, for instance, Beatrice/Hunt Foods/La Choy/Peter Pan/Aunt Nellie's (Figure 2.4) in the name of building family brand line extensions. Essentially, the corporation speaks in two voices simultaneously. More often it is one or the other, the corporate or brand identity. This is the case with Procter & Gamble, which downplays its corporate identification and instead emphasizes its brand names, which it encourages to compete with one another for market supremacy. The P&G logo is barely discernible on the package. Smaller companies building a family of products sometimes give the brand identity the priority design position in most if not all visual elements to reinforce the package design at point of purchase, but retain the name as the manufacturer's

2.4 *Beatrice*
As part of a new design system (instituted in 1983 and discontinued in 1986), Beatrice Corporation added corporate identification to existing package design of divisional brands. Both corporate and brand identity are highlighted.

Design Credit: Staff, Beatrice Foods
Photo courtesy of Jeff Rich, former design director of Beatrice

designation for legal and financial purposes, for instance, The First Years/Kiddie Products (Figure 2.5).

Aesthetics aside, not all corporate identities accomplish what they set out to do. As visible expressions of a corporation's philosophy, outlook, and culture, they sometimes mumble when they should articulate, obscure when they ought

KIDDIE PRODUCTS, INC.

2.5 *Kiddie Products, Inc.*
The First Years
Design Credit: Selame Design

to enlighten, depress when they could excite, or bore when they could just as easily stimulate.

But changing one's corporate identity is not something that lends itself to a quick yes/no decision. The idea of making a change can sometimes be spontaneous, occurring as it often does at that precise moment when management steps back and—perhaps for the first time—sees what the organization has become, where it is going, where it is strong, and where it is weak. It often finds, to its dismay, that the name it has been laboring under for many years no longer serves the best needs of the company.

This especially applies to those companies that have so radically altered their business that no one really knows who they are or what they do. Large, midsized, or small, they may have a name, but their image has become so blurred and confused that they are on the brink of becoming unrecognizable, corporate nonentities.

When that happens, the company's best friends will be too polite to tell them, and its competitors will surely say nothing. But its customers, vendors, and stockholders might—and often do.

Numerous research studies and focus-group interviews reveal that the trend to corporate facelessness is starting to confuse and irritate the very people management can least afford to offend. These negative attitudes, says Harry O'Neill, are reflected by Opinion Research's data.

"Not only is the public entitled to know as much about the companies that seek their patronage," O'Neill maintains, "but people shouldn't have such a hard time figuring out what makes one company better than the next."[4]

An even better way of putting it is the classic McGraw-Hill house ad that ostensibly promotes the value of business-to-business advertising but could just as well make an eloquent case for corporate identity (Figure 2.6).

Most managers have a pretty good instinct in sensing that something has gone awry when their sales drop, product returns mount, or the competition scores too many points at their expense. When these things happen, one can be sure management wastes little time coming to grips with the problem—and fixes it.

But when the problem is less obvious, as it often is when human perceptions are at the root, management is often slow to respond.

In far too many cases, the cause is as predictable as the effect. Hell bent on growth and expansion, management assigns a fairly low priority to such intangibles as image and identity—not having learned yet that identity can become a marketable asset as valuable as any other the company shows on its balance sheet. Perhaps even more so.

---

[4]Personal interview of Harry O'Neill by F. Peter Model.

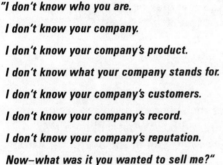

"I don't know who you are.

I don't know your company.

I don't know your company's product.

I don't know what your company stands for.

I don't know your company's customers.

I don't know your company's record.

I don't know your company's reputation.

Now—what was it you wanted to sell me?"

2.6 *McGraw-Hill*
Reproduced with permission from McGraw-Hill Publications Company

Imagery is given lip service at the corporate level. Whatever actual work needs to be done is left to the divisional heads. No one has given much thought to the "totality" aspect of corporate identity, so there is no systemized approach to applying whatever identity the company has acquired over the years.

Inevitably, the company starts giving mixed signals. There is not *one* corporate letterhead, but a baker's dozen. There is no consistency in signage. Some trucks are painted the corporate colors while others are allowed to roll around bearing the standards of the acquired company, which may have legally ceased to exist but which still holds the loyalty and affection of its workers.

Often, when such visual anarchy is brought to the attention of top management, there is deliberation—and vacillation. [This may not be the time to rock the boat. The divisions are performing well. Who cares what people say? *"Hey*, if it *ain't* broke, why fix it?"]

In fact, it *is* "broke," but the realization will not set in until someone with initiative starts collecting all the various letterheads that are being used, orders photographs of various signs and trucks and store fronts; gathers every piece of printed material that bears, or purports to bear, the company's current symbol/signature—and then, mounting all of this evidence on 20" × 20" display boards, calls management in for a look.

Until that happens, the organization is allowing itself to be held hostage by its own blurred identity—or identities, as the case may be.

What does it cost?

The first question that must be asked, after the shock of discovery wears off, is "Why doesn't it work?" The last question should be, "What will it cost?"

"Actually," observes former J.C. Penney Chairman of the Board Mil Batten, "Good design can cost *less* than bad design. That's because if you 'shop around' for the cheapest, over the long run you're likely to have bought the most expensive. What you saved going in you'll be paying a lot more trying to make it work to keep up with change."[5]

Costs are actually relative. It's not so much the design fee—which can range from a low of $5,000 to a high of $500,000, and in rare instances, more, depending on whom you use.

Thus Allegis Corp. budgeted $7.3 million advertising and publicizing its change from UAL Inc., while the all-time record $200 million chalked up by Exxon came from having to "fix" and affix the new name identity to 25,000 service stations, 22,000 oil wells, 18,000 buildings and storage facilities, 55,000 underground pipe facilities, several thousand ocean-going tankers, tank trucks, railroad tank cars—and 300 million sales slips, 11 million credit cards, and several network TV specials. Business writer John Brooks reported that the figure was so mind-boggling that Exxon management amortized the cost over several years to prevent a precipitous plunge in corporate earnings.[6]

Mil Batten will be the first to say that when it comes to restructuring identities, it's not what it costs but what it will ultimately end up saving the company

_____

[5]Personal interview of William (Mil) Batten by author.
[6]"It Will Grow On You," *The Games Players: Tales of Men and Money*, by John Brooks, Times Books, 1980.

and its shareholders. Harry Gray, retired board chairman and CEO of United Technologies, is likely to be the second to concur. The $2.5 million the diversified former aerospace company spent in 1982–1983 on changing its name from United Aircraft made it much easier to acquire other companies, including Otis Elevator of Yonkers, N.Y. and the Carrier Corp. of Syracuse, N.Y.[7]

When Batten set out to use CI to signal the transformation of Penney's from a blue-collar to a white-collar mass retailer, he knew next to nothing about corporate identity. He does now. In this respect, Batten learned on the job. Like so many other CEOs we have worked with over the years, Batten found himself deeply involved in the process of changing identities, and he looks back on this effort with a great deal of satisfaction. Now retired, he says, "Today, I wouldn't want to be connected with the old J.C. Penney Company had we not gone to a new identity. Looking back, it was a big handicap."[8]

In the beginning nine of 10 CEOs haven't the vaguest notion of what CI is all about, but then they get personally involved in its development and by the time they are through they most assuredly know what CI can do for their business. Many don't even have to wait very long for the impact.

USAir public relations director Jack King says that when he went into his bank to deposit his first paycheck bearing the new name, just four weeks after the new identity program went into effect, the teller looked up quizzically and asked, "Oh, USAir. What did you used to be?"

"I replied, 'Can't you remember?' and she thought for a moment and asked, somewhat unsure, 'Allegheny?'"[9]

By itself, a new identity will not effect change. What it can do is announce change and set into motion the forces that *lead* to change. From the very first moment the new identity gains visibility, the program is bound to accelerate change within the organization.

For example, it will encourage tighter and more coherent communications. Once CBS Inc. switched to a new stationery design, recalls design director Lou Dorfsman, "Correspondence seemed to become more concise."[10] Better yet, the network soon found it was able to cut stationery printing bills by 27 percent.

A cost-benefit analysis conducted by the Public Service Company of Colorado in 1983 projected that the utility company could expect to save over $600,000 net by standardizing all printed material, vehicles, and signage during

---

[7]"Takeover Hardball: A Tough Leader Tells How to Play the Expansion Game," by Harry Gray, *Success* Magazine, May 1987.
[8]Personal interview of William (Mil) Batten by author.
[9]Personal interview of Jack King by the author.
[10]Personal interview of Lou Dorfsman by F. Peter Model.

a five-year identity changeover program. Bendix Corporation auditors found that 36 months after its identity changeover, the company had saved $200,000 just by reducing the number of forms and invoices. And Hewlett-Packard, after standardizing its packaging, reported cutting its outlays in that area by as much as 50 percent.

Other benefits

Corporate identity can also ease the pain of mergers. The problem faced by former U.S. Treasury Secretary W. Michael Blumenthal when his Burroughs Corporation took over Sperry Corp.—displacing Digital as the world's second-largest computer company—was how to integrate the two without demoralizing the employees at either entity.

Were the newly merged company to be called Burroughs-Sperry, as many insiders had proposed, thousands of Sperry employees would have felt threatened. "It might look like a takeover," he confided to his design consultants. The new identity (Unisys = *The Power of 2*) is admittedly a compromise solution that has been roundly criticized and satirized, but as far as Mike Blumenthal is concerned, "It works well."[11]

Many companies that have adopted new identities agree that internal morale goes up dramatically after the program starts to unfold. They also say staff turnover is reduced, and that worker productivity, quality control, and recruiting improve substantially.

Among publicly held companies that have undergone identity change, the investor climate is often the first to experience improvement. Within months of United Aircraft's identity change to United Technologies reports Harry Gray, price/earnings ratios "rose dramatically."[12] This would explain why so many corporate identity changes aimed at the institutional market are first announced in full-page advertisements in the *Wall Street Journal*.

Corporate identity for non-profit companies

Corporate identity is available not only to corporations. Take the not-for-profit healthcare industry, currently comprising some 15,000 healthcare facilities, and poised for explosive growth over the next 15 years. According to the U.S. Department of Health and Human Services, some $30 billion in new capital

---

[11]"Unisys: So Far, So Good," *Business Week*, March 2, 1987; also interview of Otto (Tony) Spaeth, AGP.
[12]Harry Gray, *op. cit.*

expenditures will be required by the year 2000 to take care of a longer-living population.

Soaring medical operating costs are forcing many hospitals to pool their resources, and eventually necessitating the merger of geographically scattered units into larger-scale medical centers. Adding to their fiscal pain is the emergence of health maintenance organizations and profit-making hospitals such as the Humana chain.

The competitive threat is forcing medical administrators to do something that was unthinkable just a decade ago: *assume marketing postures.* They are rising to the challenge, committing sizable funds to modernize their physical plants, improving patient/visitor signage, and creating visibility where none existed. Systemized identity programs allow even the smaller community health centers to look progressive. They are, in effect, pumping new blood into the tired veins of aging institutions.

Schools and colleges, confronted by different challenges to their continued viability as institutions, are likewise placing greater emphasis on identity.

Even nations are finding that systemized graphics can be of immense value in making the citizenry feel better about themselves. Canada, for example, during the Pierre Trudeau administration, launched a massive, nationwide identity program designed to simplify citizen access to the often-bewildering bureaucracy.

First, it did away with all existing government nomenclature by instituting a two-word system. The Canadian Ministry of Air Transport became simply, Air Canada; the Ministry of Health & Human Services became Health Canada, etc. Then it replaced all signage with a new system keyed to a singular graphic device—the national symbol of the maple leaf.[13]

Identity as a reflection of a company's true nature

Systemized corporate identity is becoming more important, and as the world continues to shrink, no people seem better at it than the Japanese.

A little over three decades ago, to all the world the three words "Made in Japan" meant cheap rubber sandals and wind-up toys with a life expectancy of 24 hours. Today, those same words represent innovative, well-designed precision products of superior quality, often carrying an above-average price tag—and well worth it.

---

[13]In sharp contrast stands the U.S. government's identity program, or "non-program" as the National Endowment for the Arts suggest in *Raising the Standards: The Federal Graphics Improvement Program, 1972–1980.* The report reads like an indictment of bureaucratic footdragging as it reviews NEA's attempt to clean up and unify the government's bewildering array of graphics.

In 1955, Akio Morita, executive vice president of Tokyo Tsushin Kyogo KK—better known as "Totsuko"—was in West Germany, trying to interest retailers in his company's TR-55, the world's first transistor radio. Taking a break, Morita ordered a dish of ice cream at a sidewalk cafe. Intending to compliment his guest, the waiter stuck a tiny paper parasol in the ice cream. Morita was stunned. Here was confirmation that Japan had a serious image problem. He returned home and set in motion a marketing program in which industrial design and visual identity would play a pivotal role in creating a company that would make the world sit up and take notice. Totsuko became the $7 billion Sony Corporation, the very symbol of Japan Inc.

What Morita recognized that day was the realization that, sooner or later, will confront every head of a growing business: *The company has grown while its image has not.*

In the case of Totsuko, the image problem extended well beyond the company gates. To the waiter, and to others Morita called on, the novelty of a Japanese businessman footloose in Germany seemed greater than the revolutionary product he was promoting—one that, ironically, had been invented by an American company (Western Electric), which never realized the potential of its transistor until Morita's company showed them what it could do. The rest, as they say, is marketing history.

3

Questions every top-level manager will want to ask about identity

Now that we have a better idea of the importance of corporate identity, the inevitable questions must be asked: *Who? What? Where? When? Why?* And *How Much?*

- Who should initiate CI? Who will set the guidelines? Who should be in charge?
- What will it consist of? What will it do for us?
- Where will it do the most good? Where do we find the people to give us identity?
- When can we expect to see results?
- Why not just clean up what we've got? Why don't we have our advertising agency do it?
- How do we know we're not well thought of? How can we be sure our divisional people will use it? How do we work it into our advertising? How will we even know the damned thing'll be any good?
- How much are we prepared to pay for a new CI?

The questions are apt to be endless. They will go on clear through the design process, right up to and possibly through the implementation stage. They may sometimes strike even the person asking the questions as naive, but they should never be brushed off as being inconsequential.

The professionals who are called upon to answer them must never forget that the questions are usually asked by executives to whom it had never occurred that their enterprises might be made to perform better by *looking better.*

Sometimes the questions are first raised by one or more people well down the rungs of the corporate ladder—usually on some operational level where the identity problems first manifest themselves.

Although the initial discussions about identity will take place in-house, inevitably the call goes out for an outside specialist in CI. If nothing else, the involvement of a design consultant will assure management that the dialogue will not bog down in a welter of vested interests and will remain, more or less, on an objectively even keel. Unlike selecting the baby's name, which usually involves only the parents, the search for identity—at the risk of splitting metaphors—can easily become a highly charged political football game that not even the strongest-willed CEO can referee.

Once the decision is made to go for a new identity, the consultant(s), working closely with the client team, starts the design process with some basic research. The analytical work falls into two basic areas, internal and external.

Internally, the company's entire communications output is assembled for study—not just letterhead and signage but also brochures, advertising, packaging, and office forms. Staff members are interviewed to elicit their views about the organization and how it is perceived within the house.

Externally, the consultants and their researchers may contact any or all of the key publics with whom the company routinely deals—customers, vendors, distributors, retailers, investors, bankers, legislators, and community leaders. The purpose is to determine the discrepancies between real and perceived images: how the company sees itself—and how others see it.

Now the deliberations begin: The consultant and/or management groups attempt to define what sort of corporate image management would like to project, given the likelihood that how it wants to be seen may not necessarily be the way these various constituents see it. The more publics a company must deal with, the harder it is to establish consensus. Often, the hardest part of trying to create an identity is to try to distill or synthesize the myriad perceptions, real and imagined, into an acceptable goal.

Once parameters have been sketched—and at this early juncture nothing is cast in concrete—the hard issues have to be addressed. For example, does the company name have to be changed? If so, for what reasons? What can a new name for the company do that the old name doesn't? This may be the toughest question management faces, for, as we will explain later, the company's name may be its most valuable asset. The older the company, the greater its investment in the name by which it has long been recognized and on which it has built its reputation and good will.

Because a company name no longer accurately reflects its business may not be sufficient grounds to drop it. US Steel is one thing, but what if your company's name—take American Express, for example—is found to have a rock-solid global image that would suffer if a change were attempted? (As it happened, AmEx—born in the Pony Express days—was indeed found to lack relevancy, but rather than tinker with the name, the company modernized its visual identity).

To what extent should your leading brand name figure in your corporate name? Does it lend itself to the kind of "visual" translation that works as well on packaging as it does in advertising or on annual reports? Can an identity be crafted so sufficiently distinctive as to be both aurally and visually memorable?

Once an identity takes form, how will it be used to further the company's strategic and marketing objectives? Who will make sure it does so? Since consistency in use of planned identity is the key to any successful application, how can management make sure that the graphics standards are maintained?

Benefits and rewards

There is no longer any doubt that there is a clear correlation between corporate identity and productivity. It has worked for too many of the world's largest corporations to continue to be disparaged as "a con job," or as "corporate cosmetics" by those who've never tried it. Ask former Mobil chairman Rawleigh

Warner Jr.[1] Or a client of ours, Ken Rossano, Director of External Affairs at the Bank of Boston (née First National Bank of Boston):

"Before our identity change we were, and looked, fragmented and had trouble conveying to people the scope of our business. We needed an identity that would unite all our divisions under one corporate umbrella. The new CI, our customers tell us, not only looks great but meets all of our marketing objectives. Now it's less expensive to sell our banking products and services."[2]

Or his counterpart at USAir, public relations director Jack King:

"The employees who used to call Allegheny 'Agony Airlines' loved it. They regained their pride almost overnight. It was almost as if they had put on their formal clothes and gone to the prom."[3] (For more on the transformation from Allegheny to USAir see pages 43 to 45).

Or, representing companies substantially smaller than major oil companies, banks, and airlines, David F. Rowse, President of New England Apple Products Inc., Littleton, Massachusetts:

"I honestly don't believe we'd have been as successful as rapidly had we not undergone an identity change."[4]

Rowse's company is better known these days as Veryfine, a brand name it began to use as its standard bearer in 1975 as part of a massive identity overhaul. It made a huge difference, he insists.

Rowse attributes "a great deal" of the company's annual 30 percent growth rate to the new visual identity, explaining, "It has helped us lift our products out of the category of commodities and allowed us to precisely position them, and as a result get a higher price for them than ever before. It has also let us get out of the private label business and concentrate more on our branded products."

When New England Apple Products began its transformation in 1975, annual sales hovered at the $7 million mark. In 1987, sales topped $125 million.

Once management has accepted the inevitability of an identity change, and has gotten a fairly good idea of the costs that might be involved, the one question that invariably gets asked—usually out of earshot of the design consultant—is, "Why can't we handle this thing ourselves, in-house?" Or, "Why not turn it over to the *advertising agency*? What are we paying *them* for, anyway?"

The answer to the first question should be obvious: For the same reason doctors do not diagnose members of their immediate families. They may have the knowledge and skill, but they may lack objectivity.

As for the second question: The ad agency is paid to create advertising for

---

[1]Personal interview of Rawleigh Warner Jr. by author.
[2]Personal interview of Ken Rossano by author.
[3]Personal interview of Jack King by author.
[4]Personal interview of David F. Rowse by author.

the here-and-now. In the volatile advertising business, people tend not to think too far into the future.

USAir Group CEO Ed Colodny remembers that when Allegheny first began thinking of a name change, some airline staffers suggested turning the problem over to its ad agency. Colodny said no. "Ad agencies do campaigns. Designers *do graphics* and are specialists in tying together visual images."[5]

When J. Walter Thompson came on board as agency of record, they began to play an important role in helping Allegheny management define its identity problems. Thompson researchers provided proof that as "Allegheny" it would never be perceived by the flying public as a "brand-name" airline on a par with the Big Three. "I think the Thompson people were actually relieved,"[6] reported Colodny when he turned to a San Francisco design firm that had made airline identity a specialty.

"Advertising agencies," he feels, "believe advertising conquers all. Personally, I don't think they are philosophically prepared to accept any other alternatives, and will take on this kind of work only reluctantly, as a client accommodation."[7]

He may be right. Several years ago, Helmut Krone, the legendary art director of Doyle Dane Bernbach, hailed in a *Wall Street Journal* ad series for being a visionary, was quoted rather immodestly as having "spent [my] life fighting logos. Logos say, 'I'm an ad, so turn the page . . .' I just don't leave out the logo. I give the client something better."[8]

This, from the agency that gave us the Volkswagen "Beetle," which has long been the living "logo" for West Germany's so-called *Wirtschaftswunder*—its remarkable postwar economic recovery. One devoutly hopes that the day he was interviewed, Mr. Krone had his tongue in cheek, since it is an article of faith in his profession, as in ours, that any mnemonic device that triggers recall while giving the client more bang for his buck can't be all bad.

Richard S. Bartlett, Eastman Kodak's Vice President of Marketing Communications, remembers an "exchange of views" that occurred during an advertising review meeting in Rochester. In the course of an agency presentation of forthcoming ads, one of Bartlett's colleagues indicated that the Kodak identity was too small and suggested it should be more prominent. Protested the agency account executive: "But that would ruin my ad." Bartlett looked him in the eye and said, "It's not *your* ad, it's KODAK's ad, and our identity must be prominent."[9] Each

---

[5]Personal interview of Edwin I. Colodny by author.
[6]*Ibid.*
[7]*Ibid.*
[8]Helmut Krone, "The Wall Street Journal article," in *Ad Age;* 1987.
[9]Personal interview of Richard S. Bartlett by author.

time a corporate name and/or symbol is seen and recognized, the company's marketing equity increases in value. And, along with the instant recognition, according to numerous Starch leadership studies, *more* people pay attention to the ads. Not a bad return for a one-time investment in CI—even if it's not media-commissionable.

What about turning corporate identity over to those who specialize in the "engineering of public consent"—the public relations agency?

Here again, the issue of lack of objectivity must be faced, even if—unlike advertising people who are paid to create copy and art for the here-and-now—the PR people operate on far broader and wider horizons.

The problem with leaving the creation of CI to a public relations agency is more pragmatic than philosophic: with only a few exceptions, most PR firms do not have corporate identity specialists on staff. When asked to take on the CI project, they usually subcontract the work to an outside design firm, often a studio or collective of freelance commercial artists who have little or no contact with the client organization.

If the corporate insiders are often not plugged in to the deliberations of the long-term strategists, one can imagine how difficult it now becomes maintaining a dialogue through several new buffers—the PR agency account executive, who generally is not involved in creative work, relating the client's preferences to a design studio that is not even on the premises of the PR agency.

Moreover, public relations consultants tend to equate success with the number of exposures they are able to produce from month to month. Given that kind of mindset, it may be difficult for them to assign a high priority to a program that may take many months to develop before it is even ready for implementation.

At the least, *in-house* public relations or marketing communications directors such as USAir's Jack King or Eastman Kodak's Dick Bartlett enjoy a much closer and more immediate relationship with the CEO, and are often deputized to take charge of the day-to-day operations of the CI program. Thus, at AT&T, where the CI program has been in effect since the early 1970s, the most important "go/no-go" decisions in days leading up to divestiture were made by Walter Straley, then vice president of public relations, who acted as proxy for a succession of chief executives, only one of whom, H. R. Romnes, truly understood the importance of CI.[10]

Thus, at AT&T, where the CI program has been in effect since the early 1970s, the most important "go/no-go" decisions in days leading up to divestiture

---

[10]Personal interview of Thomas Ruzicka by F. Peter Model.

were made by Walter Straley, then vice president of public relations, who acted as proxy for a succession of chief executives, only one of whom, H. R. Romnes, truly understood the importance of CI.

Because of a lack of a new overall visual marketing strategy, the burden of interpretation fell upon the legal department's shoulders. Perhaps the worst thing any corporate chieftain can do, assuming he has made a commitment to upgrade the organization's profile, is to assign the CI "asset-management" operation to the legal department without a strategic visual marketing plan. Some companies that have done that justify the move by insisting that when it comes to trademark registration and protection, the legal department is the most logical liaison with the design people.[11]

It rarely works. In Boulder, Colorado, Thomas Ruzicka, who served for 18 years as AT&T's Graphic Design Manager before his retirement in 1984, well remembers his battles with the in-house legal department.

He had been brought into AT&T from Jersey Bell in 1966 to "try and bring some order out of the graphic chaos" generated by the 32 Bell telephone companies. The stop-gap program was a PR department initiative. Ruzicka does not believe top management was even aware of his presence. Consequently, "Whenever I wanted to do something, even as innocuous as trying to systemize the various Bell symbols, I kept hearing from Legal, saying, 'You can't do this' or 'You can't do that.' They thought they were protecting the crown jewels. That may have been the case, but in doing so I think they stymied change."[12]

But once Romnes committed AT&T to its multimillion dollar CI program in the early 1970s, hiring West Coast graphic specialist Saul Bass, at the suggestion of longtime industrial designer consultant Henry Dreyfuss, "The lawyers became pussycats," Ruzicka says.

What tamed the AT&T tigers was the realization that the design consultants not only had the ear of the chief executive officer, but that the CI program had been initiated at the very top of the corporate pyramid.

"Without the top-level interest," Ruzicka says, "no CI program will work. Identity is not the sort of thing that can be pushed from the bottom up."

This is not to say that to be successful every CI program requires a hands-on approach by the highest corporate official, but it helps, if only to get it properly started. Ed Colodny of USAir says, "The CEO ought to look at the design process as 'revenue production,'" and adds, "If he's the least bit curious, he also should look at it as somewhat fun."[13]

---

[11]*Ibid.*
[12]*Ibid.*
[13]Ed Colodny, cited.

Without such CEO patronage, even the strongest consultants risk having their expertise and authority undermined by underlings—or as Eliot Noyes put it to Rawleigh Warner, when he weighed going to work for Mobil in 1965 as chief design consultant, he felt he would be "Nibbled to death by ducks."[14]

Warner remembers that "(Noyes) expressed his misgivings. He said he'd undergone similar attempts to bring good design to corporate business, and had fought the good fight. He said he did not intend to take on the job for us unless I would agree to be his champion.

"That seemed like a reasonable proposition to me, and I agreed."[15] Thereafter, and for the next few years, Warner walked in lockstep with Noyes and, later, with graphic designers Ivan Chermayeff and Tom Geismar whom Noyes brought in to develop and implement the corporate identity phase.

"In the beginning," says Warner, "you'll have to spend a lot of time with the designers because the quality and effectiveness of their work is surely going to reflect the amount of top management's involvement—and I mean *involvement*, not merely 'support.'"[16]

As a result, it didn't take long for word to filter down to the lowest branch of the Mobil infrastructure about the good sense in cooperating with the design team as the program was very much "the Chairman's baby." Warner did nothing to discourage the perception. "In any organization as big as Mobil's, you'll get 9,000 reasons why something can't be done," and not all of them come from the legal department.[17]

"The trick," warns former J.C. Penney head Mil Batten, "is to avoid being perceived as a 'control-freak.'" To win the hearts and minds of the entire J.C. Penney organization, Batten had to instill the feeling in all departments "that it was *their* program, not Mil Batten's. There was too much riding on it to risk having anyone say that the program was a whim and that the only reason they had to go along was because it was the chairman's idea."[18]

Designers in the boardroom

The call for front-office involvement is actually a swing of the pendulum back to the halcyon 1930s, when such industrial designers as Noyes, Dreyfuss, Raymond Loewy, Donald Deskey, and Walter Dorwin Teague were *personally* hired by the company chief or the owner of the firm. In those days, designer and

---

[14]Rawleigh Warner, cited.
[15]*Ibid.*
[16]*Ibid.*
[17]*Ibid.*
[18]Personal interview of Mil Batten by the author.

client enjoyed a one-to-one relationship: there were no committees to serve as buffers.

In time, as the work grew in complexity, the design function became as much a marketing and political event, with designers relegated to the background. That turned out to be a mistake. Where designers are buried six layers down, left in the dark as to the corporate business plan and marketing strategy, design solutions often look like graphic exercises.

Cast adrift in a sea of caution, most designers opted to play it safe, and some now feel "We became cosmeticians." Consequently, by the 1960s many chief executive officers came to the conclusion that their staff designers couldn't be much good, so when decentralization became fashionable during the heyday of the conglomerate, recall some corporate cosmeticians, "Our group, that had inched its way to some status, suddenly found itself scattered over 15 locations, and the only time we got together was at the annual Christmas blow-out."

Over the past ten years or so, more business heads have learned to trust their instincts and to hire not only consultants with whom they feel comfortable but people who will argue forcefully for what they believe will be in the client's best interests. And they are willing once again to pay top dollar after years of looking for "bargains."

"Try and find a fellow you feel compatible with," says former Mobil CEO Rawleigh Warner. "As the head man, you are going to make the decisions, but you'll need a designer or a team of designers whose values you think are like yours. If not, you run the risk of getting somebody in, getting them to work long and hard and then having them come up with some kooky idea that you and your Board of Directors will find totally unacceptable. *That's* throwing out money. You wouldn't give *carte blanche* to the architect doing your house, would you? Think of the company as 'your house.'"

For corporate identity to live up to its promise, it has to be long-lived.

In fact, any CI program is likely to be more valuable five, ten, even 20 years after its introduction, than when it is first implemented. To reap the benefits of increased public awareness—acceptance of a new identity—the program must be responsive to the company's long-term goals and marketing strategy.

In most structured client organizations, we have learned, only a handful of people are privy to long-range planning. Fewer, still, are close enough to the very top to speak in The Master's Voice.

Another problem consultants face is how to react objectively to the inevitable territorial imperatives that are expressed in every organization, small as well as large. As frequently happens, some very good ideas from inside get pummeled or shelved because the person who first expressed them may be in disfavor or too low in the pecking order. As a result, the independent CI specialists often find themselves not just mediating warring factions but shaping long-term corporate and marketing strategies by playing the devil's advocate.

The larger the company, the more complex the program, the dicier it becomes to achieve consensus. It's the way the game is played. So when it comes to something as intangible as the way a company should alter its corporate identity, the infighting may become nasty. The in-house designed logotype that is sauce for the office in Gander, Newfoundland, may not be sauce for the plant down in Duckwater, Tennessee.

CI comes of age

As an integrated profession, now highly valued by corporate management, CI has come a long way in just under three decades.

Until the late 1950s, many businesses would entrust product design to engineers, factory and store design to local architects or contractors, brochure design to nearby ad agencies, signage to a paintshop or billboard firm, letterhead, cards, and business forms to either a local printer or stationery supplier.

Each vendor would sincerely do its very best in following instructions given, some even exercising imagination to project the client identity as they interpreted the assignment. Some would turn out all right, but many would look simply awful. Seen in its totality, the company image often would turn out to be precisely opposite to the one management had hoped to project.

"If you want to develop a good corporate identity program," insists Rawleigh Warner, "it is absolutely essential to get the best designers you can. There's not much chance you'll find such a person working for an oil company, an insurance company, or a department store. The best are likely to be in the design business. That's where we went to look for them."[19]

The keeper of the mark

Making sure that the good corporate identity program *stays* good is often the hardest part of the design process. One of the consequences of all this merger/restructuring activity is that the best-intended CI program can easily fall apart under neglect or upon the unexpected departure of key front-office personnel.

---

[19]Rawleigh Warner, cited.

This is the reason more companies these days are advised to order a Holy Writ—a manual of design standards—and appoint a central administrator to make sure everyone pays homage to it.

In the largest companies, this "keeper of the mark" reports directly to the chairman or president, and heads a staff that could be as large as Mobil's—125 in the United States alone, with another 300 coordinators overseas.

Functioning as staff coordinator for overall planning and direction of the organization's constantly evolving corporate ID and brand programs, the "keeper" power can be considerable—and indeed it ought to be.

On Mobil's Table of Organization, the post shows up under "Marketing" rather than "Executive" because, explains Rawleigh Warner, "This keeps him in the mainstream of everything that flows outward to Mobil's service stations, buildings, signage, trucks, packages and, ultimately, *customers*."[20]

"Everybody has their own idea of what looks good," says USAir's Colodny, "but if you don't start out with a design standard and develop hard and fast criteria, you'll almost certainly deviate from where you set out to go and wind up being a mixed bag. You'll also lose whatever consistency and uniformity you'd hoped to build into an identity that you bought at considerable expense."[21]

At the IBM Corporation, one of the first to make design a corporate religion, a simple, straightforward declaration of principles by the son of the founder leaves nothing to chance, and prevents communication chaos from ever taking root.

On January 26, 1961, President Thomas J. Watson Jr. issued to all home office, plant, and field office supervisors his famous one-paragraph edict that has never been amended:

> Good design is good business. Imaginative use of design helps to sell our products. Pleasant, efficient work areas contribute to better morale and productivity. Dramatic design in printed material increases its message impact. The Vice President for Design is responsible for coordinating company design activities in architecture, interiors, display, products, packaging and printed material. Since design excellence concerns all areas of the business, you should make certain that all your people are aware of its importance.[22]

Walter F. Kraus, who now manages IBM's worldwide design program, explains, "We want to be sure that the design efforts are collective and that a singular program not only focuses the character of the corporation but presents it correctly to our many publics."

---

[20]*Ibid.*
[21]Ed Colodny, cited.
[22]Thomas J. Watson, Jr., IBM Brochure; January 26, 1961.

Thus, design at IBM is a *corporate* and not a departmental responsibility, assumed by headquarters to ensure "adequate attention and unified direction" by people who understand that they have the fullest support of the President's office.

What is interesting about IBM is that it has never used a design application manual, despite its global sprawl. The company relies almost entirely on the written criteria established nearly 30 years ago by the original consultants, graphics designers Paul Rand and Eliot Noyes.

Identity crisis: the grounding of "old agony" airlines

There's nothing wrong with calling yourself Allegheny International Corp. if (a) you're based in Pittsburgh, seat of Allegheny County, (b) you used to be known as Allegheny-Ludlum Steel, and (c) you are now a thoroughly diversified holding company whose better-known brand names include Sunbeam, Wilkinson Sword, Northern Blankets, etc.

But if you're a regional airline with big ideas that happens to be headquartered in Hanger #12 at Washington D.C.'s National Airport, or if your name is Edwin I. Colodny and you like to "dress for success," Allegheny is not a very good name to keep.

This was especially true considering the fact that back in 1979, when airline deregulation took effect, supposedly freeing Allegheny to compete wing-to-wing with other major "trunk" carriers coast-to-coast, this airline—which flew to more United States cities than American, boarded several million more passengers a year than Pan-Am, and operated more daily flights than TWA—was still being thought of by many travel agents as a "businessman's commuter service," and referred to by its passengers as "Agony Airlines."

The perception was totally skewed. Having acquired Pittsburgh-based Lake Central Airlines and Utica, N.Y.-based Mohawk Airlines in the late 1960s and early 1970s, Allegheny was, in fact, the nation's sixth largest airline, serving the densest passenger market—northeast and east-central United States from Virginia north to Montreal.

In the tradition of other U.S. airlines, Allegheny—née All-American Aviation—had started business in the 1930s as a regional mail carrier. What began as a sideline by glider buff Richard C. DuPont (of the Delaware DuPonts) had gradually evolved into a "feeder," directing passenger traffic from the small towns of Maryland's eastern shore and western Pennsylvania to the "trunk" carriers operating out of New York and Washington. As it grew, Allegheny kept feeder routes under the subname "Allegheny Commuter."

"Maybe you shouldn't judge a book by its cover," says Colodny, a former Civil Aeronautics Board attorney who joined Allegheny Airlines in 1957 and ran the airline's marketing until assuming the presidency in 1975, "but one should at least make the cover interesting enough to get looked at."[23]

As early as 1971, Colodny and his boss, CEO Les Barnes, had been exploring the idea of changing the airline's identity. Research by its ad agency, J. Walter Thompson, confirmed that the regional name was counterproductive, but the ensuing ad campaign that claimed Allegheny was bigger than people assumed it to be was simply not convincing. American was "big,"; so were United and TWA. But Allegheny, a/k/a/ Agony? Colodny and Barnes agreed: the name would have to go.

And so would the existing graphics. JWT Research revealed that Allegheny's undistinguished red-white-blue "flying wedge" mark was often confused with Delta's. And the colors, when tested against such mythical names as "Union," "U.S. Air" and "Republic" (which did not actually come into being until the merger of Southern and North Central Airlines in the mid-1970s), evoked consumer images of a government-owned carrier.

The questions were "to what?" and "when?" 1974 was not a good year for big change. The country was mired in the OPEC-fueled economic recession. Congress seemed less than anxious to deregulate the airline industry and the CAB was firmly in control of route structuring. The Big Three—American, United, and TWA—were not about to welcome another carrier into their transcontinental hegemony.

So, while the other airlines watched their fuel gauges, Colodny and his PR director, Jack King, planned for the day conditions would change, as they invariably do in this cyclical industry. While Allegheny's ads continued to insist "it takes a big airline to . . ." Colodny hired San Francisco-based Landor Associates, (also responsible for the identity of carriers QANTAS, Alitalia, and British Airways) to start developing a new CI.

Over the next three years, Allegheny and Landor did all the required "prep-work" that would enable the airline to soar once industry deregulation took effect. While no name had yet been agreed upon, a new color scheme—three shades of red—had been approved. In fact, two identical, parallel design systems were being developed—one for Allegheny, the other for Airline X—so that each time Allegheny added a new facility or upgraded its ticket counters, the new color scheme was used. Forms, letterhead, baggage tickets, etc., were put on limited inventory ("planned depreciation") so that when deregulation actually took effect on January 1, 1979, all design systems would be "go."

By then, of course, Colodny had approved the name change—to USAir Group Inc. Almost immediately, it started service as far south as Louisiana and west to Arizona, expanding the network to 100 cities in 25 states.

"We wanted to be geographically established to give credibility to the name

---

[23]Ed Colodny, cited.

and image before unveiling 'USAir,'" says Colodny. "As Allegheny we'd grown but not enough to make our flying areas a main selling point."[24]

For the next nine months, the airline speeded up painting of aircraft, upgrading of ticket counters, redoing all forms and letterheads, baggage tags, signage and so forth.

"We targeted October 28, 1979, the first anniversary of President Carter's signing of the deregulation act, as the day we'd introduce our new name, new service, and overall USAir image and concept. We wanted to take advantage of the timing, refurbishing and all the hype that went along with it to really get the USAir message across.[25]

Colodny succeeded brilliantly. On October 28 more than 17,000 USAir signs were put up in airports nationwide; starter kits of new ticket stock, new rate cards, bag tags, and other print material were rushed overnight by Federal Express to travel agents along with detailed instructions to destroy anything bearing the name "Allegheny."

"By planning ahead," says Jack King, "using up a lot of material on hand and having to actually scrap very little, we achieved tremendous cost savings."[26] "Repainting the planes was the least of it, " says Colodny. "It's a 48-hour zero-expense job because planes are constantly being repainted."[27]

To inquiring trade reporters, though, Colodny denied this was anything but an image upgrading. "We have an itch to expand but we put a lot of anti-itch powder on it," he would respond.[28]

It turned out to be mere talcum powder. Now, USAir is truly up there with the majors, serving nearly 100 airports coast to coast. In 1986 and 1987, it acquired both Piedmont (making it number two in the East to Continental) and Pacific Southwest (PSA), which dominates the 350-mile San Francisco–Los Angeles air corridor with 550 daily flights.

It is likely that Piedmont as well as PSA's famous "happy face" planes will go the way of other swallowed airline identities. Colodny is a True Believer in standardized design. He remembers how things used to be when he came aboard Allegheny: "The sign painters would walk into the hangers and use the closest things they had to the current letter style."[29]

It cost Allegheny $3 million to become USAir. "Three million isn't a lot of money to a company thinking of changing its name. It's worth every cent we spent. In fact, it was a bargain."[30] (Figures 3.1– 3.7)

---

[24]*Ibid.*
[25]*Ibid.*
[26]Jack King, cited.
[27]Ed Colodny, cited.
[28]*Ibid.*
[29]*Ibid.*
[30]*Ibid.*

3.1 *USAir*
What will the new name look like?

3.2 *USAir*
A selection is made.

3.3 *USAir*
A theme is developed.

3.4 *USAir*
A new look for the fleet.

The aircraft take on a newfound feeling of pride as the new dress code is applied.

3.5 *USAir*
A new look at point of purchase.

The closest view of an airline's identity is often at the ticket counter.

3.6 *USAir*
More than meets the eye.

An identity program is a total statement and as such must . . .

44

3.7 *USAir*
Goodbye, Agony; Hello, USAir:

Airline CEO Edwin I. Colodny (left) and design consultant John Diefenbach of Walter Landor Associates, at Washington, D.C.'s National Airport, the carrier's home base. Change-over was trumpeted by a major ad campaign.

The game of
the name

San Francisco conglomerateur John Beckett faced an identity crisis a number of years ago. He admitted as much in a full-page *Wall Street Journal* ad:

> I run a company called Transamerica.
> By almost any yardstick it's one of the biggest on the Big Board.
> So what happens when I'm introduced to a new face?
> "Transamerica? Oh yes, the airline . . . "
> If we wanted to be known as an airline, we'd have bought one.

A year later, Transamerica did just that, when Kirk Kerkorian sold Beckett his Transinternational charter. It only aggravated Transamerica's identity crisis.*

Transamerica was founded as a holding company in 1928 by the legendary A. P. Giannini for his Bank of America and sundry other financial units. For the next 30 years, Transamerica became so powerful in the west that it was always warring with the federal government. With the passage of the restrictive 1956 Bank Holding Company Act, Transamerica was told to divest itself of banking and find a new line of work.

If there was ever a perfect time for a name change, that was it. But in the late 1950s Big Business had not yet learned to appreciate the value of a positive visual identity; nor did it realize that a good name should be treated as a corporate asset, a bad one as a liability.

Under Jack Beckett, the "new" Transamerica emerged by acquiring such service-oriented companies as Occidental Life, the country's ninth largest insurer; Budget Rent-a-Car, third largest; and the jewel in his crown, United Artists, founded in 1919 by Mary Pickford, Douglas Fairbanks, Charlie Chaplin, and D. W. Griffith.

Just on UA's theatrical grosses alone Transamerica should have been a hot issue on Wall Street. But as Beckett's ad suggested, its recognition value—on a scale of 10—was somewhere between 0.5 and 1.0.

A design firm was brought in. It developed the distinctive "T" logo still in use, as well as a proprietary typestyle. Though the new graphic identifier was used by all the subsidiaries—especially the film company—it was not done consistently. Thus, recall studies showed a 67 percent recognition rating for the name

---

*Not to be confused with Trans World Airlines, which in 1960 acquired Hilton International hotels, Canteen Corp., and Century 21 real estate. In 1983, troubled Transworld Corp. spun off TWA (now owned by arbitrageur Carl Icahn) and in 1986 liquidated itself. All that remains is a shell, TW Services housing a food service and retirement care company.

"Transamerica," but only 18 percent knew what Transamerica did for a living. Beckett seemed leery of forcing the moneymaking subsidiaries to surrender their individual identities.

He would come to rue that decision in 1980 when United Artists sought to break away from Transamerica. UA had been acquired in 1967, not merely because it was immensely profitable, but also because, in contrast to Transamerica, UA was highly visible. When Beckett rejected the separation bid, UA chairman Robert Benjamin and President Arthur B. Krim left to set up Orion Pictures—taking with them virtually the entire management team and most of the talent and properties under contract.*

By this time, of course, Wall Street knew all about Transamerica. The corporate persona that failed to come through in print did so *architecturally:* its controversial, 48-story pyramid headquarters dominated the San Francisco skyline and cast its shadow all the way east.

The Benjamin and Krim walkout posed a structural threat, so Beckett called a meeting of their successors to tell them that he wanted to impose the corporate identity; in effect, *kill* UA.

Steven Bach, then head of production, recalls pleading with Beckett. "I reminded him it was the only major Hollywood studio founded by creative people and that with all due respect to his needs at that moment, the company would *not* smell as sweet bearing the name of a financial institution."

Bach pointed out that Paramount hadn't been renamed Gulf + Western Pictures, and then he got to the heart of the matter. "By changing the name to Transamerica Films, you (Beckett) will say to the creative community only that *the corporation regards itself as more important than the tradition behind it and the people who make the product that makes the money.* It's not the name *per se.* It's what *changing* the name implies about the company's *attitude towards the people who do the work.* And if they don't question the attitude, the press will. Loudly."[1]

Although Transamerica has since deconglomerated into an insurance and financial services firm, in a way Jack Beckett was a man ahead of his time. In his ambivalence toward corporate/divisional identity, he first raised the question that is only now being addressed by many chief executive officers: when does a "holding" company have to start projecting itself like an "operating" company?

---

*Transamerica's movie problems resolved themselves when UA collapsed as a result of the $36-million debacle, the making of Michael Cimino's *Heaven's Gate.* UA assets, mainly its film library, were sold to Metro-Goldwyn-Mayer, which then changed its name to MGM/UA. But Leo the Lion no longer roars over the lot in Culver City: it's now owned by Lorimar, the TV company.
[1]Steven Bach, *Final Cut,* William Morrow, 1984.

NOTES ON THE NEW CORPORATE ETYMOLOGY

"A trademark should be short, vigorous, incapable of being misspelled to an extent that will destroy its identity; and—in order to satisfy trademark laws—*it must mean nothing.*"

George Eastman was looking for a name to give his newest invention, the world's first portable camera. The $25 device came with enough rolled film for 100 pictures; when the role was finished, the customer would ship the sealed camera back to the Eastman Dry Plate & Film Company in Rochester, N.Y., where technicians would remove the exposed film, have it developed, insert a new roll, and send everything back to the customer—all for $10.

Here was truly a unique product, deserving a unique name. So Eastman invented that, too. He had an affinity for *K*—"a strong incisive sort of letter"—and looked for a name that would begin and end with *K*. He shuffled vowels and consonants into dozens of variations until he got what he wanted—*Kodak.*

Back home in Rochester in 1888, Eastman was regarded as something of an eccentric. Today, his gambit is becoming standard operating procedure both in naming products and in renaming companies. Only today computers do in a few hours what took Eastman weeks to do: create a proprietary name that cannot be found in any dictionary and that will be legally unassailable in any potential trademark infringement suit.

By feeding the computer morphemes—the smallest work unit with any meaning—the computer will link or bracket them with a variety of prefixes and suffixes and spew out an assortment of mellifluous-sounding names that mean only what the users want them to mean.

Companies interested in trying out constructional English on their own IBM-compatible PCs can now do so by mail order. Salinon Corporation, a Dallas software firm, has developed "naming disks" that will "create names based on the image and meanings you desire."

The program, costing less than $500, can satisfy three common naming needs: (1) *Names that are unknown* but sound like English language words (e.g., Zipad, Corloon), (2) *Names composed of Greek, Latin, or English root parts* (e.g., AquaFlow, AutoDoc), and (3) *Names strung together from existing words* (e.g., Munchy Krunchy Mint Cookies, SeaSurf Smorgasbord). And while Salinon claims the program triggers an alarm whenever it encounters a profane or scatological name, the drawback is that you'll still have to test out the name to see if it works, and then call in a graphics consultant to implement the name into your CI system.

For Salinon, as for consultants like Ira Bachrach of NameLab (which specializes in brand-naming, e.g., Compaq, Acura, etc.), business couldn't be better. Computer-naming has gotten to be a $250 million a year sub-industry, and future growth is assured as long as industry stays in a state of flux.

The U.S. Patent Office estimated in 1987 that over the next 12 months it processed 30,000 more new name applications than it did ten years ago. In 1986, there were nearly 80,000 submissions.

Yet, some identity-consultants are becoming troubled by what they see taking place.

Many grew up believing that names are at the heart of the corporate or brand identity, and that too much use of "constructional English" may be dehumanizing the corporation and simultaneously neutering the products at point-of-sale.

"There are times when I feel like Mork from Ork getting my instructions from HAL," says a former Yale lexicographer—referring to the early '80s TV sitcom about a humanoid refugee from a planet where all the emotions have been bred out of the populace, as well as to the diabolically fiendish computer in Stanley Kubrick's film *2001.*

This name-consultant, who wisely wants to remain nameless, says, "The public thinks it's a game. If it is, it's a game with no real winners, just compromises. It's also debasing the language."

The trend to hybrid names and acronyms also seems to be discomfiting those CEOs who are called to explain just how these meaningless names will enhance profits or add substance to the corporate image.

Every once in a while, the question crops up at shareholder meetings as *ex post facto* approval is sought to adopt a new name. Most of the time, the design work will already be underway. A Wall Street gadfly explains: "Management does not expect any opposition from the floor. Most people really don't care under what name the company does business, just as long as it makes profits."

Most name consultants react stoically to the criticism, and regard the public razzing they've been getting from the media as almost inevitable. Lippincott & Margulies' Clive Chajet says, "It seldom lasts very long." Walter [Margulies] used to reassure skittish clients that "these things usually blow over in less than two months."

In an article in *Crain's New York Business,* whose publisher is one of the most vocal critics of corporate hieroglyphics, Chajet correctly pointed out that "these instant reactions focus on the subjective aspects of the

names themselves," instead of clients taking the long-range view and wait-
ing to see if they work.[2]

One L&M change that ran into heavy flak when it first appeared was
NYNEX, the new name for one of the seven new operating companies that
emerged out of the AT&T's divestiture. At the time, Margulies agreed that
to someone hearing NYNEX for the first time, "It might have sounded like
a cough medicine"—a remark that did not go unnoticed in the wider
reaches of the old Bell system.

The letters N, Y, N, and E stood for the New York and New England
Telephone companies that had merged, while the X, NYNEX director of
corporate ID Joseph Kayal stoutly maintains, "stands for Excellence."

Unlike BellSouth, Bell Atlantic, and Southwestern Bell, the combined
New York and New England companies wanted nothing in their new
name to remind Wall Street that they were once part of a regulated industry. Reason: they needed heavy private sector financing and thus could not
be perceived as a utility. Says Clive Chajet: "we had to move them away
from the meter-reading mentality."[3]

It worked. Today NYNEX is ranked as one of the more profitable of
the "Baby Bells."

In today's volatile, market-driven economy, the answer is: the minute it
decides consumers are as important an audience for the corporate identity/mes-
sage as security analysts.

But as Richard J. Ferris can bitterly attest, there's a *caveat:* before you
start tinkering with the identity, be sure to get the full and unqualified backing
of your Board of Directors; and try to avoid picking a name that engenders
controversy.

Ferris is the former board chairman of UAL Inc.—née United Airlines Inc.—
the Chicago-based holding company for a number of travel-related units, the two
biggest being United Airlines and Westin Hotels. He lost his job largely because
the corporate identity change he engineered both galvanized and unified the
opposition to his long-term growth plan for the company, and made it ripe either
for takeover or breakup.

In February 1987, after a two-year $2.3-billion acquisition binge that added

[2]"Parting Shot," Rance Crain, *Ad Age,* 1984.
[3]"New York Intelligencer," *New York* magazine, March 9, 1987.

Hertz rental cars, Hilton International, and other travel-related companies to UAL's corporate portfolio, Ferris announced that the $10 billion company would shortly change its name to Allegis Corporation—a computer-derivative of the root words "allegiance" (loyalty) and "aegis" (protection).

Six weeks later Ferris resigned. His supporters were in disarray, his master plan was in shreds. The $7.3 million budgeted for the UAL/Allegis switch would not be spent; all advertising was halted and the board announced that after selling off the hotels and car rental units, the company would once again be known as United Airlines Inc.

Ferris's ambition was to build a travel supermarket for frequent flyers and turn them into one-stop shoppers. It galled him that businesspeople who would book United drove with Avis and Budget and stayed at Sheraton, Four Seasons, and Holiday Corp. hotels. One call to UAL's Apollo computer would do it all.

As corporate strategies went, it was brilliant—in theory. And an identity change would clearly help get the point across to Wall Street that the company had become much more than an airline and that there was no reason for continuing to give the stock such a low price/earnings ratio. Again, in theory.

Timing can be crucial

While it was true that the name Allegis—pronounced *uh-LEE-jiz*—was hardly descriptive of travel, it would be specious even at this point to ascribe Ferris's fall to merely having picked an inappropriate name. Chances are that *any* name would have unleashed the demon forces that brought him down. The worst Wall Street could find to say about Allegis was that it was "confusing." (Drexel Burnham Lambert airline analyst Helane Becker spoke for many when she questioned management's need to explain its proper pronunciation. She asked, "If you have to tell people how to pronounce it, do you really want to call yourself *that?*")[4]

Still, there's no question that by agreeing to a name that invited instant ridicule and derision, Ferris *drew attention* to a major corporate restructuring before it was fully in place and before he had won over his critics.

They proved a formidable lot. Inside the organization, Ferris faced a *putsch* by the United Airlines pilots; from outside, by corporate investors skeptical of

---

[4] Helane Becker, *New York Times*, Feb. 19, 1987.

Ferris's synergistic scheme. The pilots, resentful of Ferris's two-tier salary struc-
ture, had gone to Wall Street for help in turning United into an employee-owned
airline. One investor who liked the idea was flamboyant New York realtor Donald J. Trump—no slouch at playing the name game (Trump Tower, Trump Plaza,
Trump's Castle, etc., etc., etc.) After buying more than 5 percent of Allegis's
stock, Trump was widely quoted as saying the new name "sounded like the next
world-class disease." With that remark, Allegis as a potential takeover issue was
"put into play."

"The name change," Trump later explained, "made me more militant as an
investor and more willing to speak out against management, because I thought it
was so wrong." He adds, "I think it brought out even more anger at management
and made a lot of people say they had finally had it."[5]

Ironically, the stock price nearly doubled—but not for the reasons Ferris had
hoped. His defensive strategy entailed a $3-billion recapitalization, and as the alle-
giance of the directors began to wane, Ferris soon lost their aegis. It became clear
to the board that Allegis was worth more were it to be broken up. Thus, Westin,
which cost UAL $52 million in 1970, will probably fetch 20 times as much;
Hertz, bought in 1985 for $587 million, twice as much, according to Wall Street
assessors.

The new conservatism in corporate identity

The Allegis debacle sent monentary shock waves through the corporate identity
industry in much the same way the Edsel traumatized Detroit back in the late
1950s. In time, it may even have a salutary effect on the business, slowing down
the unhappy trend to "re-identify" established companies with hybrid, often
unpronounceable names. Instead, we may now see more companies retaining
their *old* names and making more creative and imaginative use of them—concen-
trating instead on updating their logos and symbols.

But it will not be an overnight development. It will take some doing to buck
the trend to change for the sake of change. Items:

• Since 1980, well *over half the companies included in the latest list of Fortune
1,000 Largest Companies* have undergone *restructuring* of one kind or another

• In 1986 alone, *more than 4,000 companies, large, medium, and small—worth
an aggregate $190 billion—merged.*

---

[5]"Air Pockets Around United," *Time* magazine, April 20, 1987; also Associated Press, April 14, 1987.

As a result of all this corporate fermentation:

- Nearly *790 of these were among the 1,382 companies that changed their names in 1986*, a 30 percent increase over 1985.
- By 1987, 12 of the 65 companies that comprise the Dow Jones Composite Index had changed their names.

Here are just some of the more recent ones, with the original name shown in parentheses:

ABEX (American Brake Shoe & Foundry Corp.), AMAX (American Metal Climax), ARMTEK (Armstrong Rubber Co.), AMTRAK (National Railroad Passenger Service), CSX (Seaboard Coast Lines/Chessie System), USX (United States Steel), ENRON (Houston Natural Gas), UNUM (Union Mutual Life Insurance), NYNEX (New York & New England Telephone), UNISYS (Burroughs and Sperry computers), COMPAQ (Gateway Computers), Maxus (Diamond Shamrock), PRIMERICA (American Can Co.), GENCORP (General Tire & Rubber), NAVISTAR (International Harvester), TRINOVA (Libbey-Owens-Ford)—which, one "amused columnist" points out, sounds like a delicatessen owner's recommendation of the day—or the most perplexing name change of all, MBPXL (Missouri Beef Packers), since acquired by Cargill Inc.

What's behind this new corporate etymology? Are these odd new names really necessary? Why are so many old-line companies willing to dispose of years of equity and goodwill in order to take on nomenclature that even the new owners have a hard time explaining?

More to the point, are these names effective communicators? It depends on where your interests lie. For all their grumbling, Wall Street analysts no longer think the names are all that terrible. In February 1987, a curious *Wall Street Journal* reporter studied the performance of those companies that had changed their names and found many of them to be outperforming the Standard & Poor's 500 Index.

UNISYS was up 18 percent in market value since the name change, USX was up 28 percent, TRINOVA up 24 percent. Explains one analyst: "If the fundamentals are there, a bad name won't hurt, and if they're not there, no name will matter." To prove the point, Figgie International, cited in Chapter 2 as not being particularly inspiring, has outperformed the S&P by a whopping 213 percent.

All that may be true, but there's more to changing identities than pumping up P/E multiples. Consider Sara Lee Corp., which until March 1985 was known as Consolidated Foods Corp. Its S&P value is up 60 percent, yet in 1986, when the BBDO advertising agency asked Chicago area consumers whether they were aware of this name change, 95 percent said they weren't.

Does this mean the millions of dollars American business now spends on recasting its corporate identities are being frittered away on what even Ferris of United Airlines admits is often seen as "a frivolous exercise to amuse columnists and incite phoneticists"?

Certainly not. The decision to change a well-established identity or name is hardly a casual one. No corporate manager accountable to others—family, outside directors, shareholders, or customers—would risk substituting an unknown name without good reason, and based on valid research, for one that has become highly esteemed over the years.

A ROSE BY ANY OTHER NAME?

William Shakespeare's Othello might have lived longer had he gone into corporate identity consulting: "He that filches from me my good name robs me of that which not enriches him, and . . . makes me poor indeed."

In days of old, companies and often brands were named after their founders as a way of assuring customers that some*body*—not a faceless factory—stood behind the product. Often, they featured their likenesses.

Clean-shaven King C. Gillette did so when he introduced the first disposable safety razor in 1895. So did the bearded Smith brothers of Poughkeepsie, N.Y.

The sons of a restaurateur whose homecooked candies were promoted as a cure-all for diners "afflicted with hoarseness, coughs or colds" had taken their father's sideline and built it into a thriving business. Soon bogus drops began appearing under the name of "Schmitt Brothers," "Smythe Sisters," even some "Smith Brothers" no one had ever heard of.

4.1 *Smith Brothers'*

To nip competitors in their buds, the brothers put their rotogravured likenesses on the little bags, which is why today William is known as "Trade" and Andrew as "Mark" (Figure 4.1).

Robert J. Corr wishes it were that simple today. In 1980, the Adolph Coors brewery of Golden, Colorado, tried to sue him for "trademark infringement and unfair competition." Two years earlier, Corr (rhymes with "oar") went into the natural sparkling soda business in Chicago. By the time he heard from Coors (rhymes with "tours") he'd built a $4 million business.

Coors, a $1 billion company, sought to convince the courts that Corr's Natural Beverages, Inc., willfully set out to cut into its market, even suggesting Corr was not the defendant's real name. But Corr triumphed over Coors when it defied the brewer to produce a single Chicagoan who'd willingly swap a can of Coors beer for a can of Corr's soda water. Beer for a soda? The case was thrown out, but not before Corr ran up a hefty legal bill (Figure 4.2).

4.2 *Coors/Corr*

Then there's New York realtor Henry A. Lambert. He turned a hobby for Italian home cooking into a very profitable business—a $16 million chain of nine trendy New York retail shops and seven restaurants called "Pasta & Cheese." When it got to be too big, he sold it to Nestlé's Carnation Co. He changed his mind and bought back the shops, but was stunned to learn he couldn't get the "Pasta & Cheese" name back. He had title *only* to the unique *typestyle* used on the package signature. "Henry made a classic mistake," says his friend David Liederman, of David's Cookies. "You don't name a company after your generic product. You have to give it an *identity*. He'd have won had he called it *Henry Lambert*'s Pasta & Cheese." His new chain will be called "August's"—after Lambert's middle name.[6]

There's no question that in a depersonalized consumer marketplace, those companies blessed with a recognizable name or signature hold a clearcut advantage over enterprises whose images have been compressed into nonhumanistic symbols or obtuse acronyms. But don't take our word for it: ask Estée Lauder, or Debbie Fields, the cookie lady.

In today's market-driven corporate world, the operating company's reputation is constantly on the line. It's not how well the company performs on Wall Street, but on Main Street—and where it stands on *quality, service,* and *delivery.*

Ferris of UAL acknowledged as much when he said Allegis won't mean very much in the foreseeable future, any more than "Xerox" did when Chester Carlson and Joseph C. Wilson on the Haloid Corporation first introduced the name in 1958.

"It's up to us, management and employees, to make it mean what we want to make it mean," stated Ferris.

As to the failure of Consolidated Foods to make its new name register, all that means is that the bakers at Sara Lee, after pouring their dough into the name-blender, didn't do or spend enough on communicating the change to their publics. It may be hard to prove, but consider how effectively Japan's Nissan Motors went about keeping its American dealers in the corral while informing the car-buying public of its decision to kill the Datsun name and replace it with *Nissan.*

The car maker's logic was unassailable. Nissan was caught in a competitive squeeze. Having been the first Japanese carmaker to open up the North American market, it found itself handicapped fighting rivals Honda and Toyota with a name only used here and nowhere else. Old line Datsun dealers at first were furious, seeing years of missionary work going down the proverbial greasepit. But their

---

[6]"New York Intelligencer," *New York* Magazine, March 9, 1987.

fury was short lived: because of the massive $30 million worth of saturation advertising and publicity Nissan put behind the name change, public awareness of the new name jumped from 2 percent to 17 percent in just three months. By the fourth month, most people had forgotten the name Datsun.

Heavy advertising support also enabled Black & Decker Manufacturing Co. to quickly absorb and market, under the B&D name, more than 175 GE products in 12 different appliance categories. Only, unlike Nissan's ditching of the Datsun name, B&D couldn't just overnight jettison the immensely popular GE name. Here's what happened.

Around the time B&D was discovering the joys of niche marketing with their Dustbuster portable vacuums, GE management got set to pull the plug on its Housewares Group. With a 2 percent return on sales, small appliances no longer fit GE's long-term growth strategy, and it became one of the 232 businesses GE had shed since 1980.

By acquiring GE's Housewares Group, B&D in one fell swoop would become the nation's leading small appliance firm—assuming it could transfer the "loyalty equity" GE had built up over more than 50 years. This was easier said than done, since GE's powerful name and logo would still prevail in the same housewares department where B&D hoped to be dominant.

Black & Decker did so by dropping the word "Manufacturing" from its corporate name, developing a striking new company and product-wide visual identity system so as to repackage not only its own lines but also the ones that had long borne the GE identity. The idea was to deliberately blur the lines separating B&D from GE, and vice versa. For instance, 60-second TV spots featured, back to back, 30-second commercials touting such cordless products as an eggbeater from GE and a portable emergency light from B&D.

Soon, few customers could tell which product was whose. Eventually, B&D owned up to what it was doing. The magazine ad for a B&D-acquired automatic steam iron was typical, headlined, "Mother Told Me Never Buy Anything but a GE Iron. Which Is Why I Bought a Black & Decker."

The big question that today's builders of tomorrow's industrial empires ought to ask themselves is whether some of the new names now altering the corporate skyline will be the IBMs, Coca-Colas, or Sonys of the future. It's not an easy one to answer.

"You have to decide whether or not the investment you have in the name you now have outweighs changing,"[7] observes USAir Group's board chairman Ed Colodny. Allegheny had really little choice: it could not have taken on such cosmic name brands as American, United, Pan American, and Transworld under

---

[7]Personal interview of Edwin I. Colodny by author.

its regional name. USAir not only met the marketing criteria but was also easy to remember.

It was Colodny who had come up with the name, although he encouraged Landor Associates, Allegheny's design consultants, to come up with other, possibly better names. They couldn't.

"USAir says several things at once," he explains. "It says it's the United States. It's big, a name that suggests stability. It's a generic name, like United or American but it's not Eastern, Western or Northwest."[8]

And what has it done for the company? Since 1979, USAir Group, Inc. has nearly quadrupled its passenger mile volume and route system, partly due to its acquisition of two major regionals—Piedmont in the East, and PSA in the West.

A good name is hard to find

Companies that undergo restructuring and downsizing and in the process are forced to also dispose of their traditional names, admittedly do not have an easy time coming up with suitable alternatives. These days there are few majestic names left that have not yet been copyrighted or trademarked.

"All the good ones seem to be taken" has become the CEO's universal complaint, and it's no exaggeration. Etymologist Victoria Newfeld, Editor-in-chief of *Webster's New World Dictionary*, confirms that "almost every word" in the latest edition seems to be spoken for. Even a name like XYLYX (from the Greek root word "xyl" = wood) which a Pacific northwest lumber company coveted, was taken.[9]

In 1977, the frustration in finding a suitable name that would satisfy his trademark attorneys and not require customers to swallow their tongues pronouncing it drove a Palo Alto electronics engineer to name his new microwave theft alarm company SOLFAN Systems. When a *San José Mercury-News* business reporter asked the entrepreneur what Solfan stood for, he earnestly replied, "Sick-Of-Looking-For-Another-Name."

Since the early 1980s, American Can has undergone a gradual transformation from a packaging company to a financial services conglomerate. In 1985, life and health insurance, mutual funds management, mortgage banking, syndication, and specialty retailing accounted for 80 percent of its profits. Former Wall Street "whiz kid" Gerald Tsai Jr. sought to make it 100 percent of American Can's profits and in 1986 he disposed of the packaging division. But the buyer, Triangle

[8]Personal interview of Edwin I. Colodny by author.
[9]Victoria Newfield, *New York Times*, February 19, 1987.

Industries, insisted that the deal include rights to the company's 86-year-old name.

Tsai was partial to the letter X but his design consultants—arguing the marketplace was glutted with X-names—persuaded him to opt for a name like "Amcan" that would retain some of the "American" equity, but the lawyers said no, that would make Triangle unhappy. Out of a long list of 400 candidates, Tsai finally agreed to go with "Primerica," even though some of his associates thought it might make the company sound like a meatpacker.

If Tsai had had his way, he says he wouldn't have gotten involved in the name process. The only reason he did, a friend thinks, was to make sure his associates wouldn't pick "an improper name." He was afraid of being ridiculed, as so many others have been.

When should one *not* change a company name? There is no hard and fast answer to that, as no two situations are ever quite the same. Generally, no change is called for when the old name is not a misnomer and when it does not retard growth by conjuring up negative stereotypes. One school of thought holds that if the name "dates" the company, then perhaps the company ought to find a more contemporary substitute. But as we have seen in the case of American Express, the worldwide strength of the name precluded finding something better. Like Wells Fargo bank and Western Union telegraph, American Express has become an institutionalized name—shorthand for credit cards and traveler's cheques, in much the same way "Xerox" is generally taken to mean "photocopy." (We will say more about *that* problem in our examination of trademarks in Chapter 5.)

The Bendix Corporation illustrates a situation where good public opinion research was able to spare management the expense of making unnecessary change.

DIVINE INSPIRATION, 99 AND 44/100 PERCENT PURE

The second-best known brand name—after Coca-Cola—was discovered in church.

In 1878 there was an accident at the Cincinnati factory of William Procter and James Gamble. On a lunchbreak, a worker left the soap vats churning, whipping extra air into the liquid. To cover his tracks, the workman said nothing, so his supervisors were none the wiser until orders starting coming in for "the soap that floats." Procter's son Harley, a sales manager, gave the serendipitous product a further edge by ordering each cake to be notched. This would give customers the feeling that they were buying two bars for the price of one.

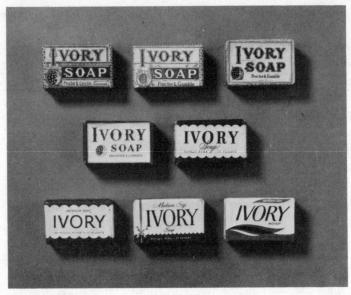

4.3 *Ivory*
From 1898 to today, there have been a number of variations in packaging design, but the name has endured.

But he still needed a name. "White Soap" lacked magic. It came to him one Sunday morning during church services, as the minister took the congregation through the 45th Psalm ("All thy garments smell of myrrh, and aloes, and cassia, out of the ivory palaces, where they have made thee glad.")

Selecting *Ivory* was 99 and 44/100 percent pure inspiration. It was also born of human judgment. The spiritual connection might have eluded a 1987 computer but not Harley T. Procter as he sat in his pew: what, he must have asked himself, is closer to Godliness than cleanliness (Figure 4.3)?

Long after Bendix sold off its washing machine business to low-profile White Consolidated Industries, opinion research showed that not many of the people it hoped to influence were even aware that Bendix was now into sophisticated electronics for the automotive industry and was also a Pentagon contractor. There was nothing wrong with the Bendix name. In fact, it retained much of the goodwill it had built up in the 1930s. The problem, analysis revealed, lay in the company's failure to communicate to industry how it had restructured itself and the results of its expansion. It was a case of "Out of sight, out of mind."

COMEnergy

COMElectric

COMGas

COMMONWEALTH
GAS COMPANY

4.4 *COMEnergy*

Before New England Gas & Electric Association became Commonwealth Energy System in 1980, the Bay State utility group was often perceived as a regional trade association. ComEnergy CEO Gerald A. Anderson describes it as "a nightmare. Massachusetts is renowned for its provincialism. We used to get tear-stained letters from customers on Cape Cod who hated paying their bills to a New Bedford utility. It really irritated people."

Regrouping various local utilities into two divisions—gas and electric—permitted abbreviation of the existing gas company's Commonwealth name and three distinctive color-coded symbols as the visual solution to a politically troublesome situation.

Design Credit: Selame Design

Once the problem was identified, corrective measures were taken. There was no need to change the Bendix name.

A different sort of name problem confronted the Singer Company of Stamford, Connecticut, a few years ago. Unlike American Can, International Harvester, and Libby-Owens-Ford, which not only sold off their primary businesses but their historic brand names, Singer's restructuring allowed it to have its cake and eat it, too. It spun off its 135-year-old sewing machine operation but refused to sell the hallowed Singer name.

Singer's late CEO Joe Flavin felt his company had too much invested in the name to let it go and preferred instead to spend as much as $10 million on an advertising/public relations campaign aimed at its various publics. The multimedia push explained why Singer pulled out of the home sewing market and why its aerospace, defense electronics, and postal metering operations would continue under the Singer name.

Flavin did admit the ad campaign cost far more than a name change might have.

Sometimes a little name change will go a long way.

In mid-1986, with no fanfare, Gulf + Western Industries changed its name to Gulf + Western Inc. Since the 1983 death of its flamboyant founder, conglomerateur Charles Bluhdorn, G+W had dramatically gone from being a madcap acquirer to a seller of more than 65 subsidiaries valued at over $4 billion—"heavy metal" industries as well as extensive hotel and sugar-refining operations in the Dominican Republic.

The surviving "industries" were not very industrial: motion pictures (Paramount), publishing (Simon & Schuster and Prentice Hall), sports (Madison Square Garden, the New York Knicks, and New York Rangers), and financial services (Associates Commercial Corp.).

Under Bluhdorn's successor, Martin Davis, G+W had become more stable and profitable. Yet, insiders worried that the company might still be perceived as it was under his unpredictable predecessor. A name change seemed logical.

Management called in several CI consultants for their advice. In the meantime, an external audit conducted by the financial relations department revealed the company enjoyed a surprisingly strong following on Wall Street, and that it might risk losing visibility by abandoning the G+W name. In contrast to Bendix, G+W had done an excellent job communicating vast changes that were taking place to the publics that mattered most.

"We finally concluded the solution lay practically in our laps," says corporate communications vice president Jerry Sherman. We simply lopped off the word *Industries*."[10]

As it turned out, the cost of change was negligible: the leisure-time subsidiaries had all kept their own identities, which bore the postscript legend, "a Gulf + Western Company"; old letterhead continued to be used until it ran out, and then was replaced with the truncated signature.

Actually, the G+W case is not so unusual. The vast upheaval that has been taking place in the way America does business both here and abroad has forced many to adjust their nomenclature, or abandon it altogether for brand-new identities.

[10]Personal interview of Jerry Sherman by F. Peter Model.

5

Ten basic rules
for playing the
game of names

In April 1987, two New York area firms announced they had changed their corporate names. American Can Corp. had become Primerica Corp. following a major restructuring program, part of which entailed selling off its old name along with its packaging business. "After all," explained its big two-page ad in *The New York Times*, "it doesn't make much sense to go on calling yourself American Can when you no longer make cans."

A few weeks before, that same paper carried a one-paragraph item to the effect that the North Pole Refrigeration Corp. of Brooklyn had changed its name to the South Pole Refrigeration Corp. When the company was asked by phone what seismic event lay behind this sea change, an official there snapped, "It's none of your damned business," and hung up.

Why the new name? North Pole to South Pole is obviously no improvement, unless one happens to switch from servicing walruses to penguins. Like many bigger corporate name changes these days, it made no sense.

How can you tell whether a name is "bad"? What makes a name "good"? Who judges? By what criteria?

We offer the following "home rules" of the naming game, as well as amplifying comments.

RULE # 1

Changing names "for the sake of change," without first establishing valid grounds for change, may only blur an established corporate identity and dilute the residual value of a good name.

A "good" name is one that works, has worked in the past, and quite likely will continue to work in the future with little or no modification.

For a long time the management of a group of nursing homes for the elderly was well served by the name "Extendicare." Then came the nursing home scandals of the 1960s and Wall Street began steering investors clear of that industry. Though Extendicare was never implicated, its stock plummeted.

After changing its name to *Humana Inc.*, the Louisville, Kentucky-based company quit the nursing home industry and entered a new field—managing health-care facilities and operating for-profit hospitals. With money coming in, Humana was also able to entice mechanical heart pioneer Dr. Robert J. Jarvik to quit Utah Medical Center and move his headline-making surgical team to Kentucky.

In this case, clearly, the answer to the question "Who judges?" is the people to whom the new name conjures up feelings of trust and confidence, including physicians. And in that respect, the name, as an integral part of the corporate identity, carries with it the responsibility to deliver (not just promise) "people-care."

RULE # 2

Don't assume that a name change will solve your identity crises. You may only be looking at the tip of the proverbial iceberg. Your work may have only begun.

In the weeks following the nationwide panic generated by a rash of cyanide poisonings caused by willful product tampering with capsules of Tylenol, Johnson & Johnson management came quite close to pulling the plug on its top-selling analgesic, scrapping the name forever, and starting anew. But CEO James Burke first wanted to make sure about how people thought about Tylenol. He ordered intensive field and attitudinal research among retailers and consumers.

It turned out to be a prudent decision. Playback revealed an astonishingly high level of consumer confidence in J&J and in the Tylenol name, regardless of the continuing headlines. Consumer trust in the company barely wavered; consumers also admired the levelheadedness and candor of management in dealing with the media. Tylenol would remain; the monies that had been allocated toward a massive brand-name replacement instead went to pay for promoting the new sealed package program introducing Tylenol caplets.

In the midwest, an even touchier situation—the AIDS (Acquired Immune Deficiency Syndrome) pandemic—forced Town Mutual Insurance Co. of Des Moines, Iowa, to make its *second* corporate name change in 15 years. In the mid-1960s, it had assumed the name of AID Insurance Company—"You know, 'aid' as in 'help,' 'assistance,'"[1] company president John Adams points out. Late in 1986, it reluctantly rechristened itself The Allied Group.

---

[1]John Adams, *Marketing News*, February 28, 1986.

RULE # 3

Corporate names carry heavier work loads than brand names, and must be approached differently.

In addition to identifying the entity, they must also:

- Burnish the corporate culture, being visually consistent in or on every application.
- Instill confidence in all supporters of the corporation, particularly vendors, wholesalers, bankers, and attorneys.
- Assure the financial community of stability.
- Inspire loyalty of all who work at/for the company, and invoke respect from suppliers, subcontractors, middle-men.
- Travel well in all languages spoken within the company's sphere of operations.

Additionally, the corporate name should assist executive campus recruiters and "headhunters" and develop pride among staff and workers to raise morale and productivity levels.

In foreign countries where the company does business, the corporate name should generate respect, not condemnation, and lend support to indigenous operations without falling into idiomatic traps. Example: during Esso's computer search for a new name, and before it picked Exxon, the name *Enco* popped out. Management considered it, but then discarded it when translators found that in Japanese, "enco" refers to "stalled car."

Mistakes crop up at home too. One of the names proposed by Lippincott & Margulies for Houston Natural Gas/InterNorth (*née* Houston Natural Gas) was ENTERON. The prefex "en" stood for energy, "on" paid homage to Exxon and Chevron, while the "ter" bridged the two. However, *enteron* also happens to be anatomical talk for the alimentary canal—"hardly appropriate for a producer of natural gas," sniffed a spokesman for the client, which then settled for ENRON.

Global reach poses an even greater challenge to *brand*-naming. While visual identities can be "read" in virtually any language, brand-names can't.

A brand name, which occasionally will be so strong it will double as the corporate name, carries additional burdens. Brand names serve to identify brands and help consumers remember those brands. They convey the nature of the products, their specific benefits, categories, often the kind of consumers for whom they are intended. Brand names, as we will see later on in this book, ensure the products become uniquely those of the manufacturer or distributor.

The brand name must therefore be:

- Easy to pronounce, because if consumers find it hard to ask for the product by name, they won't. This used to be a problem faced mainly by packaged goods, like *Jhirmack* hair products. Now it's something makers of such capital items like cars have to worry about. Mitsubishi Motor Sales of America needed a name for a new import that "would make consumers think our car was precise and accurate." "Acura" had already been appropriated by Honda.* Mitsubishi picked Precis but then worried about pronunciation: the French way is *PRAY-see* while the American is *pray-SIS.* Ad manager Frances Oda says, "We are instructing our dealers to all say *PREE-sus* the same way."

- Easy to read, preferably phonetically (which is why the soothing balm is called Ben-Gay and not "Bengue" (Figure 5.1).

5.1 *Ben-Gay*
Package Design Credit: Coleman, LiPuma, Segal & Morrill

---

*Spelled with one "c" not two, and pronounced *ah-Kew-ra* not *AKKU-rah.* Name specialist Ira Bach-rach of NameLab proposed two c's to simplify pronunciation but was vetoed by Honda in Japan because (a) it needed a global name and (b) a double 'cc' is hard to say in many languages.

- Easy to recall, which is why South Korea's Hyundai car ads in all media, even outdoor, point out, "It rhymes with Sunday."
- Appropriately descriptive of the product, as for example, Brown & Williamson's Kool Mentholated cigarettes, Dow's Handi-Wrap plastic sheeting, or Sony's Walkman.*
- Associated with positive experiences, for example, Colonial Provision Co.'s Fenway Franks—a supermarket version of the same hot dog Colonial sells at Fenway Park, home to Boston's Red Sox (the package even carried the Red Sox logo) (Figure 5.2).

5.2 *Fenway Franks*
Design Credit: Selame Design

---

*Walkman was a name born of necessity. Originally, it was introduced in the U.S. as "Soundabout," in Britain as "Stowaway," and in Sweden as "Freestyle." But when competitors began copycatting the miniature audio tape player, Sony decided to come up with a unified name, package design, and an international warranty system. "Our English-speaking subsidiaries at first protested," Sony's Akio Morita recalls, "fearing they couldn't sell a product with an ungrammatical name like 'Walkman.'" Morita himself would have preferred the more descriptive "Walking Stereo" but also bowed to his colleagues. "Sales proved the wisdom of their decision," he says in typical Zen understatement.

- Suggestive of design treatment. Appropriate design plays a critical psychological role in developing identity (examples: the Scotch plaid used for 3M's Scotch-brand tape).

Sometimes a brand name will suggest an accompanying picture trademark ("Green Giant") that can be advantageously used in packaging and displays (Hanes' L'eggs) (Figures 5.3, 5.4).

Corporate and brand names continue to proliferate, and most of the time, for good reason. A change of name can reposition a company positively in the minds of both professional investors and consumers who must constantly be reassured that the company that wants their money is also responsive to their changing needs and lifestyles.

Yet, the question keeps being asked: how and when can we determine that a name is *not* effective and should be changed?

The answer: *when that name is perceived as tired, ineffectual, and not indicative of what the company is really all about.*

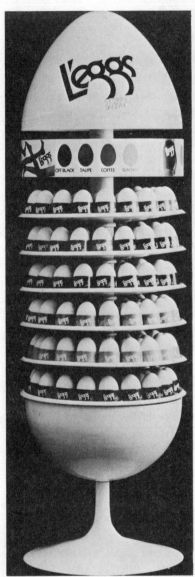

5.3 *Green Giant*
Package Design Credit: Gerstman & Meyers

5.4 *L'eggs: Hanes Corporation*
Design Credit: Roger Ferriter, Herb Lubalin.
Structural display: Howard/Marlboro

RULE # 4

When the brand name happens to be better-known than the corporate name, it sometimes pays to take advantage of that fact. An ineffective name has a detrimental effect on virtually every phase of operations, and has probably kept your company from realizing its full potential.

The Green Shoe Manufacturing Co. of Cambridge, Massachusetts, did not make green shoes; rather it is justly famous for its Stride-Rite children's line, which is why it changed its name to the Stride-Rite Corporation.

Back in 1916, another family business—Upton Machine Co. of St. Joseph, Michigan, agreed to become Sears, Roebuck's sole supplier of Kenmore washing machines. In 1947, with Sears' blessings, the Uptons introduced a Kenmore "clone" under the name of Whirlpool.

It did so extraordinarily well that three years later, Upton changed its name to Whirlpool. Under its new identity—enhanced by its now-famous whirlpool symbol—the company outgrew St. Joseph, built a sprawling plant in nearby Benton Harbor, moved into the manufacture of air conditioners (a co-venture with RCA) as well as kitchen ranges. Meanwhile, it continued to make washer-dryers for Sears, and even toyed with TV sets for Sears until the Japanese made Sears a better offer. As Whirlpool, the company became more attuned to the public than it had been as an Original Equipment Manufacturer (OEM) supplier to Sears, was one of the first U.S. manufacturers to set up a toll-free "consumer hot-line."

Unlike Stride-Rite, Sara Lee was only one of many famous brands produced and marketed by Consolidated Foods—e.g., Shasta soft drinks, Hillshire Farms and Jimmy Dean's sausages, Booth's frozen seafood, Haines and Hollywood health foods, Popsicles, and also Electrolux vacuum cleaners, Fuller Brushes, Bali bras, Hanes underwear and L'eggs, etc.

But when $8 billion (sales) Consolidated tired of its industrial-strength name, its design consultants looked no further than the number one preparer of frozen baked goods in America, the Deerfield, Illinois-based Kitchens of Sara Lee, acquired in 1956.

The Sara Lee marketing people were not enthusiastic about the switch, feeling the ups and down of the stock market could negatively affect their brand image, but they were overruled by management. A Sara Lee Corporation spokesman says, "It gives us immediate recognition on Wall Street and other areas without us having to spend millions to get that recognition across."*

But the Sara Lee approach wouldn't work for every company. Take Tampax Inc. of Lake Success, N.Y. Since 1936, it has been the leading manufacturer of tampons, but in the early 1980s, its market dominance began slipping as such broad-gauged packaged goods giants as Johnson & Johnson and Procter & Gamble entered the feminine hygiene products field. Its survival as a single-product company could no longer be taken for granted.

The identity consultants proposed the new corporate name of *Tambrands Inc.* and management agreed to it. Explained a company spokeswoman: "The Tampax name posed an insurmountable problem, since all packaged goods must carry the manufacturer's name. Tell me, would you buy Tampax toothpaste?"

A different kind of "insurmountable problem" faced New York savings banker Jerome R. McDougal a few years ago. At the time, his bank was called the Harlem Savings Bank, and he says, "Changing our name to Apple Bank for Savings was positively the best thing that ever happened to this bank."[2]

McDougal remembered what happened in 1982, when the Harlem—founded in 1855 in Harlem, then one of Manhattan's more affluent neighborhoods—tried opening a branch in a posh Long Island suburb. It received lots of brick bats—literally.

"We had to replace the plate-glass window seven times. The community sent us a powerful message that the name 'Harlem Savings Bank' was unwelcome. The geographical connotation concerning the name put us face to face with a decision. We had to ask ourselves who we were, what we were, and what we wanted to be."[3]

It was then that McDougal asked Selame Design to develop a new name and identity. Within a month after the shiny new Apple CI was introduced in 1983, nearly 5,000 new accounts were opened (three times the normal rate) and savings grew almost 10 percent by $116 million (versus a $26 million loss for a corresponding period just one year earlier).

A successful public stock offering and merger with Eastern Savings in late 1986 brought assets up to $2.7 billion from its $1 billion base prior to the identity change. Early in 1987, it returned to the Long Island community that had earlier

---

*But not in Cleveland, home since 1926 of a salad-dressing maker called Sar-A-Lee Inc. "We get a lot of half-baked calls from people who think we're in the bread business," says CEO Ralph Kovel, who is also a noted authority on collectibles. His company does $22 million a year, Sara Lee Corp.—$8 billion, so Kovel won't sue for trademark infringement. "They haven't hurt me, and I haven't hurt them."
[2]Personal interview of Jerome R. McDougal by author.
[3]*Ibid.*

5.5 *Harlem Savings Bank*
Former sign.

5.6
Jerome MacDougal introducing new name and identity.

5.7 *Apple Bank for Savings*

Corporate Name and Design Credit: Selame Design

5.8 New identity announcement card, brochures, collateral.

Design Credit: Selame Design

spurned its presence, adding $54 million in new deposits. "In terms of continuity and growth, it was the bank's most important business decision,"[4] McDougal asserts. (See Figures 5.5, 5.6, 5.7, 5.8.)

The motivation doesn't have to be as dramatic as having your storefronts smashed by hooligans. The danger signals can be much subtler: sales turn sluggish, accounts receivable start running past 90 days; quality control starts to slacken, as does employee morale. The personnel department receives fewer job applications and the stock price keeps slipping. Competition spurs unaccountably and worse, the Word is out. The company is no longer perceived as vital, as it once was.

---

[4]*Ibid.*

RULE # 5

Old and tired company names may not be related to age or fatigue; they may be old and tired because of their design. Unless they are rejuvenated, that feeling will infect the corporate culture.

Drive through California's Silicon Valley, North Carolina's Research Triangle, or along Boston's Route 128, and you will see the signs: new enterprises that are on the cutting edge of high technology but which—intentionally or otherwise—hide their powers under an opaque umbrella of clichés.

A recent compilation of business-to-business advertisers lists 295 companies whose name begins with either "U.S." or "American;" 70 firms with "International" in their titles, 114 with "General," 112 with "United," and 162 with "National."

Substituting newer words such as "Orbital" or "Intergalactic" would make no difference. It would merely compound the felony. Unless such names truly stand for something meaningful or relevant, they stand a good chance of being dismissed as contrivances, of projecting negative images that only becloud the corporate identity even further.

RULE # 6

Don't allow the company to be "sold" on a name change if there is no need to make a change.

For years now identity consultants have been approaching the J.M. Smucker jam and jelly people in Ohio, trying to convince them their name is a liability. Quite the contrary: Smucker management has made an asset out of the presumed liability through its advertising slogan, "With a name like Smucker's, it's got to be good."

"The decision to change a well-established identity cannot be taken lightly," observed the late Walter P. Margulies of the design firm he co-founded with Gordon Lippincott after World War II. In the July/August 1977 issue of *Harvard Business Review*, Margulies wrote, "It would seem foolhardy for a corporation to substitute an unknown name for one that has become highly esteemed by the public and by the business and financial communities."[5]

---

[5]Walter Margulies, *Harvard Business Review*, "Make the Most of Your Corporate Identity," July-Aug. 1977.

RULE # 7

If you have a good name, treasure it as you would your own. Use it constantly and neither misuse or abuse it.

It is a lesson learned too late by fashion designer Roy Halston Frowick, whose middle name bespoke a fashion empire that has by now seen many masters come and go. Designers often try and stretch their incomes by licensing their names to other manufacturers, usually for a 5–7 percent royalty. Halston wanted more, so in 1973 he sold *Halston Limited* to his friend, David Mahoney of the Norton Simon conglomerate, for $6 million. For Norton Simon's newly acquired Max Factor division, Halston created his still (after 17 years) best-selling men's and women's fragrances and commissioned sculptor Elsa Peretti to design the famous teardrop smoky brown bottles; next he designed a low-priced dress line for J.C. Penney's, which—to no one's suprise but his own—cost Halston the coveted Bergdorf Goodman account after 20 years.

Meanwhile, Norton Simon Inc. was acquired by Esmark (formerly Swift & Co.), which (a) ousted Halston's patron, David Mahoney, and (b) relegated Halston Enterprises to the International Playtex bra and girdle division, where it clearly didn't belong. Less than a year later, Esmark itself was gobbled up by Beatrice. Halston's imperious style clashed with the bread-and-butter Beatrice style and the designer was asked to take an extended vacation. During his absence, Beatrice began dismantling Halston Enterprises, seeking to retain only the fragrance and the J.C. Penney lines.

Then Beatrice underwent a leveraged buy-out. As part of the inevitable restructuring, Halston fragrances and Max Factor went to Revlon, itself a restructured company. Upshot: Halston came back from "vacation," was given a $1-million-a-year contract that keeps him from talking and, worse, from using even his God-given name on any new products he might want to design. He is now, as *The New York Times* called him in an allusion to Neil Simon's hit play, *The Prisoner of Seventh Avenue.*

RULE # 8

Don't be misled by the term "the name game" by making it an employees' contest. If you do, there won't be any winners, only compromises.

Just because some very large firms do it doesn't make it right. As Jerry McDougal of Apple Bank says, "A name change should involve careful deliberation; it is not an election. You've got to want [a name change] to appreciate it."[6]

He remembers that at one point during the long search for an appropriate name, the Harlem Savings Bank directors contemplated throwing it open to an employees' contest. McDougal said no. "It would have been an indication that it doesn't make any difference what your name is." Moreover, even if a winner were picked from, "say, 3,000 submissions, that contest will create ill will among 2,999 losers."[7]

This possibility must have occurred after-the-fact to the public-relations people at Burroughs Corporation when they received over 30,000 entries for a name for the new company formed by Burroughs' acquisition of Sperry Corp.

A prize of $5,000 was offered by Burroughs CEO Mike Blumenthal, who knew only that he did not want to retain either name.

Most of the submissions were trite and unimaginative. Many tried the acronym approach, i.e., BUSPER, SUPERBUR, while others let their fingers do the walking over their PC keyboards: BUSYNEX, COMPEX, WEXCO, CORTEX, each more meaningless than the next.

The "winning" name—UNISYS—is actually a contraction of "United Information Systems."

---

[6]Personal Interview of Jerome McDougal by author.
[7]*Ibid.*

RULE # 9

Professional treatment begins with hiring professionals. Creative experience counts, but what counts for even more is the consultant's objectivity and understanding of how the corporation works and thinks.

Corporations, like the people they employ, often suffer from identity crises, but treating a business takes much less time than conventional individual psychotherapy. Be prepared to pay more than $75 per hour for what will probably be a team effort involving a number of specialists—not all of them graphic designers.

Among the disciplines that may also have to be brought to bear on the problem are: demographic and motivational research, logic/linguistics, ocular measurement, industrial design, trademark/patent law, marketing, architecture, and package engineering.

On the client side, the process should start with a realization that something has gone awry. Before seeking "treatment," it is always advisable—indeed, smart—to conduct a thorough audit of your communications. As already noted, this entails gathering all of the company's visual communications materials and then, carefully, patiently, and objectively, examining them for strengths and weaknesses.

As will be shown, in a number of instances where the corporate name was at first found to be flawed, such research pointed to a problem area that had no bearing whatsoever on the identity.

As in psychological therapy, the management/patient must start out trusting the consultant/therapist, and must bring to the sessions an open mind as well as the discomfiting feeling that something's not right with the way the company is perceived.

RULE # 10

Do not allow the final selection of a name to be a solitary decision. Corporations may not be democracies but by the same token they should not operate as dictatorships.

At least, not when it comes to a name change. The name change decision may be one of the most important ones a sitting CEO will ever make, since the commitment is one the company will have to live with long after the CEO has left the company.

These days, all of the better name changes result from a collective effort involving various members of client management with specific oversight responsibilities.

Design consultants therefore should be hired not only on the basis of their past expertise with, or recommendations by, other clients, but also for their ability and willingness at all times to be *objective, dispassionate,* and *analytical*— three attributes few involved clients can be expected to bring to the conference table.

As Mobil's Rawleigh Warner points out, management should beware the *prima donna* consultants who insist on *carte blanche.* The best designers are those who give careful consideration to the stated (as well as unstated) concerns and needs of the client management team. It's important that the client listen to his own people, as well. But in the final analysis, the decision on choice of a name rests solely with the person who runs the organization.

Perhaps the choice was easier when companies were smaller and run more tightly by one man, and when there were fewer "like-sounding" names in use. Easier, perhaps, but not necessarily better. Not many names arbitrarily chosen have turned out as well as the one chosen in 1936 by David H. McConnell. To celebrate the 50th anniversary of his California Perfume Company, McConnell— who'd begun as a door-to-door bookseller but found it more profitable to sell the cologne he had been giving away as door-openers to housewives—decided his company needed something less regional-sounding. A Shakespeare buff, McConnell found his inspiration on a pilgrimage to the town of Stratford-on-Avon. Today, the company McConnell built—Avon Products—is the world's largest cosmetics firm.

A PAN-GLOBAL NIGHTMARE

It's not so much the language as the idiom that gives the brand managers of multinationals nightmares, and has led some of them reluctantly to abandon their pan-global one-brand marketing programs and return to a worldwide corporate ID umbrella sheltering a multiplicity of brands.

Gillette is typical. It markets over 800 different products in 200 countries, some of which—like India—speak as many as 16 sublanguages.

In the People's Republic of China, Coca-Cola had to rename its top-selling soft drink something other than Coca-Cola, which read as "Bite the wax tadpole." (Its new name now reads as "May the mouth rejoice.")

In Japan, Gulf Oil's "No-Nox" leaded gasoline was dropped because when pronounced "nonok" it is slang for female private parts; Sunbeam had to rename its Mist-Stick hair curling item after it was discovered "mist" is German for human excrement. S.C. Johnson's Pledge was to have been introduced in Holland as *Pliz* but wasn't because the Dutch give the soft *Z* a hard *S* sound. In parts of Latin America, Colgate is pronounced *Col-gah-TAY*, meaning "Go hang yourself." In Mexico, GM's Chevrolet division had to re-introduce the *Caribe* when it learned the original name, Nova, was pronounced No-VAH, or "no-go." In Hong Kong, McDonald's has scrapped Chicken McNuggets in favor of McChickens, for reasons that have something to do with the inability of most Cantonese to pronounce "McN" as against "McCh," while up in Canada, they no longer push "Big Macs" because that's street slang for big breasts.

Now the translation problem has come home. Bert Valencia, Assistant Marketing Professor at Texas Tech. U., recently alerted Frank Perdue that his famous slogan, "It Takes a Tough Man To Make a Tender Chicken," doesn't play so well in the burgeoning Hispanic market. It had been translated literally onto packages and in ads aimed at Hispanics, and was read as "It Takes a Sexually Excited Man to Make a Chicken Affectionate."

One does not always have to create a new name from scratch to get a new name. If you are put off by computer-constructed names, take another look at your present nomenclature.

Does it lend itself to manipulation? Can something be made of the name—an acronym, perhaps? Would initializing make the descriptor less industry-specific? Is the name compressible?

Here are some of the ways others have managed to change their names so that they are still partially recognizable to people who grew up with the old name. Better yet, by utilizing parts of their old names, the law of precedence will enable them to contest trademark/name challenges better: they got there first. (New names are italicized.)

Few people ever called it Continental Telephone Co., so switching to *CONTEL* required no consumer education. Likewise, the metal smelting industries never bothered with the mouth-filling American Smelting and Refining Company, hence *ASARCO*. Ditto *ALCOA*, formerly known as Aluminum Company of America.

When Hart, Schaffner & Marx diversified from men's suits to a variety of other clothing labels and accessories (Christian Dior, Sansabelt, Gleneagles rainwear, Nino Cerruti ties) HS&M became *HARTMARX*. With the original founders all dead, it was permissible to drop Schaffner.

Some companies don't want to go 100 percent bland because packaged goods consumers sometimes think of brand name manufacturers as "family." So they will keep the name and switch generic suffixes. Hershey Chocolate Co., now producing San Giorgio spaghetti, Luden's cough drops, and Friendly's ice cream and hamburgers, has become *HERSHEY FOODS*. With tobacco companies seeing the handwriting on the surgeon general's wall and deemphasizing tobacco if not dropping it altogether, Liggett & Myers became *THE LIGGETT GROUP*, R.J. Reynolds became *RJR NABISCO* (after merging with Standard Brands, dropping that name but retaining that of the former National Biscuit Company). *American Tobacco* (Lucky Strikes, but also James Beam whiskey, Sunshine Biscuits, Duffy-Mott apple products, Swingline staplers, etc.) is now *AMERICAN BRANDS*. When the principals of General Felt Industries bought their favorite restaurant, New York's legendary "21 Club," they didn't quite know how it would fit into their collection of interior design companies, which included Color Tile, Knoll International, and another oddity, Sheller-Globe marine insurance. Though "21" was the jewel, the name that carried the most weight, apparently, was that of furniture designers Hans and Florence Knoll. General Felt recently adopted the encircled K logo and renamed the works, *KNOLL INTERNATIONAL HOLDINGS LTD.*

Another proven practice is to *initialize*. For those companies who long ago began using their initials in their own external communications, the name switch is at best a formality. Among these we would place GE, IBM, RCA, CBS, GM, ITT, GTE, PPG, CPC, NCR. All monogram well. However, when initials create a possible word, such as GAF (General Aniline & Film Co. a/k/a ANSCO), BAT (British American Tobacco Co.) or UOP (Universal Oil Products), they open the door to derogatory meanings by others.

Word initializing can be fraught with unforeseen pitfalls such as in the unhappy case of Universal Oil Products. In the mid-1970s, it recast itself as the UOP Corporation. Try to pronounce that! Then, it erred by playing on its own weakness. In full-page financial section ads, it asked, "What is a UOP?" By the time the campaign ended, Wall Street wasn't any the wiser. But UOP management must have been.

Symbolic logic:
trademarks
and logos

A simple graphic symbol can become a powerful and compelling device for motivating large groups of people.

Think of the Stars and Stripes, the Hammer and Sickle, the Swastika, or the Red Cross. Each one triggers an instant mental reaction, for better or for worse. What the eye perceives, the mind believes.

From time immemorial, people have fought wars under symbols, waged peace under symbols, sold products under symbols, and just plain worshipped symbols. They still do, only now some call the symbols "logos"—short for logotypes—and logos are being used in print and TV advertising to sell products, services, and the corporations themselves.

We live in an age of visual symbolism, of fast-moving images. We get our factual information on the run, in quick "bites" doled out by TV anchors, condensed in newspapers like *USA Today* (whose sidewalk vending machines were deliberately designed to look like TV sets). Yet people seldom realize to what extent their lives are governed by symbols or how totally they depend on them as assurances of quality.

Symbols are often deprecated as "mere labels." But without labels to guide us—in the store or in the voting booth—decision-making would be all that much harder and time-consuming. Symbols serve as visual shorthand.*

Webster's New World Compact Dictionary defines symbol as "(an) object, mark, etc. that represents another object, an idea, etc." It defines a *trademark* as "a symbol used by business to identify goods and services by origin and manufacturer and to distinguish them from competing goods and services."

Though the two words are used interchangeably, their true functions differ. Where one serves to *inspire and rally*, the other plays a more prosaic role: it *protects.*

What characterizes a successful corporate symbol or trademark is its innate simplicity, its ability to communicate quickly what the seller wants the buyer to know—a mix of product information and corporate aura. There is, for example, no mistaking the nature of OshKosh B'Gosh's business: overalls. Its unique name within the familiar denim patch label incorporates a legend of trust: "The Genuine Article Since 1895" (Figure 6.1). Seeing how well its shares are doing on Wall Street, we are again reminded of the importance of adding "face" to otherwise faceless corporations.

"Less is more," wrote the world-renowned architect Ludwig Mies van der Rohe. The aphorism, intended to apply to building design, applies equally to graphic symbols. *The less the eye has to take in, the more the mind will store and remember.*

---

*It is interesting how many corporations still draw their names from symbols: *Tiger* International, *Star* Markets, *Sun* Energy, *Apple* Bank, *Vulcan* Materials, *Zenith* Electronics, *Giant* Food, *Caterpillar* Tractor, *Nike* shoes, *Phoenix* Mutual Assurance, *Owl* Cork & Seal, *Diamond Shamrock*, etc.

6.1 *OshKosh B'Gosh*

The retrieval process is bi-directional: just as a symbol can evoke a name or a word, so can a word or name evoke a memorable symbol. Prove it to yourself by engaging in some word-picture association.

The name Red Cross automatically conjures up the familiar mark of the organization. The Izod label will almost certainly evoke the image of the world-famous alligator. The initials CBS trigger the ubiquitous Eye.

Or try this. You are traveling down a road lined on both sides by strip malls and free-standing fast food stores when you feel the first hunger pangs. So accustomed have you become to symbols that, *instinctively*, your peripheral vision looks for familiar signs: McDonald's Golden Arches, Kentucky Fried Chicken's big striped bucket, Mister Donut's abstract little baker. While your taste buds are idling, your eyes are in overdrive.

Need gas? You search for reassuring signs—the Texaco star, the Amoco torch, the scalloped Shell, the double xx's of Exxon, the 3-D CITGO triangle. Again, the point is, you don't look for names, but for signals.

The more ubiquitous the symbol, the more effective it becomes as a mnemonic device. Few are better at utilizing symbols in this way than the Japanese. Witness the worldwide use, and impact, of the three-diamond symbol of Mitsubishi (Figure 6.2).

Although Mitsubishi is no longer the unitary organization it was before and during World War II, but instead is a $130 billion conglomerate of more than 50 independent companies in electronics, petrochemicals, textiles, food processing, automotive, pulp and paper, metals and myriad other industries, to the world it appears as one—and its symbol is the mark of quality.

So highly valued is the three-diamond symbol (which goes back to the 1870s when it first appeared on the ship's flag of fishing magnate Yataro Iwasaki) that even Lee Iacocca was willing to subordinate Chrysler's pentagon star symbol to Mitsubishi's diamonds on the cars Chrysler is now importing to the United States.*

---

*Diamonds seem to be very symbolic to the Japanese. Sony's Akio Morita, asked to explain the company's long-standing aversion to discounting, often says, "we are selling 'diamonds.' Real diamonds. We are not selling cheap paste."

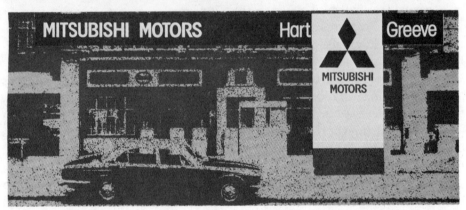

6.2 *Mitsubishi*

From mackerel to motor cars, Mitsubishi is the most known company in Japan, with over 25,000 different products.

"Mitsubishi" in Japanese means "three diamonds" and can be seen everywhere in Japan: in neon over Tokyo's Ginsa, on banks, on gas station signs along country roads, oil storage tanks, factories, automobiles, elevators, air conditioners, electric fans, radios, television sets, and textile products. The three-diamond mark is becoming increasingly familiar globally as well.

Coutts Bank

6.3 *Coutts Bank*
One of the oldest banking institutions in London, The House of
Coutts (1692), used a house mark of three crowns for its iden-
tity. It is in use to this day.

Like symbols, trademarks have been around since the dawn of civilization. In 1921, a Swedish archaeological team discovered signed ceramics in Yang-Shao-ts'un (Hunan) dating back to 4000 B.C. They are the first known trademarked goods in recorded history.

During the reign of King Solomon, Phoenician quarry workers painted unique signs of origin on the stone blocks in vermillion paint to prove their wage claims. In Egypt, it was the custom of Nile brickmasters to mark their output with what we today call pictographs; and in what might be the first private branded product, Nebuchadnezzar had his name stamped on every brick earmarked for his new palace.

Trademarks dating back to various periods and parts of the Roman Empire have been found on lead pipes, marble friezes, glassware, bronze goblets, gold- and silverware, even on lava-preserved bread loaves unearthed at Pompeii.

In medieval times, artisans began using trademarks as warranties. Then someone must have proposed using them as advertisements. In time, the mark of quality became as important as the product itself. In the present age of Gucci and similar upscale image purveyors, it still is.*

After Europe emerged from the Black Plague, the powerful guilds used the marks as a means of maintaining these "closed shops" and protecting their hegemony over the silver, gold, linen, and wool trades. (See Figure 6.3.)

During the late 18th and early 19th centuries, as innkeeping became Big Business, coats of arms were hung over the sidewalks to draw traffic. Many of these heraldic come-ons boasted of royal appointments. The monks who ran most of the breweries followed suit, marking the birth of testimonial advertising.

---

*Bottega Veneto, a rival Italian leathergoods designer and merchant to Gucci's, works the other side of the snobbery street by offering product that does not promote its name. Its slogan: "When your initials are enough . . ."

With the Industrial Revolution, a new—and mean—kind of competition sprang up among rival manufacturers. Many were resolved the old-fashioned way, but increasingly, satisfaction was sought in court. Inevitably, the trademark became a legal instrument.

Congressional passage of the first U.S. trademark registration law in 1870 set the stage for the creation of the Patent & Trademark Registration office, which is now a unit of the Commerce Department.

In 1877, the Quaker Oats Company of Chicago became one of the first registrants, when it trademarked the Quaker Man.* Prudential's Rock of Gibraltar made its debut in 1896. General Electric's (now just plain GE) symbol dates back to the 1892 merger of Thomson-Houston Light and Thomas Alva Edison's Electric Light Company. In its present "de-squiggled" form, it emphasizes the continuity of a great historic enterprise. So does Nabisco's corner tab with its replica of a 15th Century double cross—the mark of the Society of Printers in Venice. It first appeared as a trademarked *seal* to advertise National Biscuit Company's patented air-tight Uneeda cracker box.

America, more than any other nation, has had a long and sentimental attachment to human and animal symbols. By definition they almost qualify as mascots— perhaps the earliest attempt of corporations to project themselves as "user-friendly." Indeed, generations of Americans have come to regard the Quaker Oats man, Betty Crocker, Aunt Jemima, the Jolly Green Giant, Chiquita Banana and the Morton Salt Girl ("It never rains, it pours") as their trusted friends.

Cognizant of the power of symbols, most consumer-oriented companies tend to treat their mascots with loving care, keeping them contemporary as evidenced by the newly slimmed down Campbell Kids. Even in these unsentimental times, few are willing to alienate the public by doing away with them. When they do so, it should be for sound marketing reasons.

Thus, Glenmore Distilleries Co., after 52 years of continuous use on bottler labels, premiums and its best-selling 316-page drink recipe *Bartender's Guide,* has finally retired Old Mr. Boston—after consumer research showed little if any consumer awareness of the top-hatted Brahman dandy or the liqueurs he represented among the young drinkers Glenmore is wooing with fruitier, less potent "fun drinks."

Glenmore's market researchers found that Mr. Boston (the prefix "Old" had

---

*Since 1915, the object of a continuing campaign by the Society of Friends (Quakers) to forbid the "naming of religious denomination" on consumer packaging. The Friends at one time even lobbied Congress to pass a law, but the bill never made it out of committee. Sporadic attempts are still being made on a state-wide level, with no success so far.

been dropped in the 1970s) was evocative of "heritage" and "quality" but, according to the company officials, "lacked spunk." By renaming the line just plain "Boston" and sending the old gentleman to the lockers, Glenmore thinks it will "make consumers think of the city-on-the-Charles with all its colleges and the TV show 'Cheers'"—in short, *fun.*

While one famous figure of the 1930s exited, another returned when Borden Co. had second thoughts about its famous "Elsie the Cow." Elsie had been more or less retired since 1969 when the dairy company restructured itself and moved from New York City to Columbus, Ohio—there to concentrate on chemicals and to acquire a spate of snack foods companies. Elsie continued to be used by the reduced dairy division, whose loyalists derided the new corporate symbol (a nondescript oval) as a "toilet seat." The bovine face that, according to a 40-ish Gallup Poll, had been more famous than Albert Einstein's, was now rarely seen. "It is inappropriate to put a symbol for natural wholesomeness on chemical packaging," a Borden spokesman insists. True enough, but now Elsie's back, if not on chemical drums, then at least as a "living logo" that the dairy people will use in store promotions.

One of the oldest and best-loved trademarks still in use is "Nipper," the little dog listening quizzically to "His Master's Voice" coming out of the brass horn of a "Victrola."

The dog had been adopted in Bristol, England, by French landscape painter Francis Barraud, who first painted "Nipper" cocking his ears to the sound of the cylindrical phonograph. The Gramophone Company, a small manufacturer, saw commercial possibilities in the painting but requested Barraud paint over the cylindrical machine and replace it with one playing *flat* records.

"Nipper" died in 1895, six years before the Gramophone Company sold the trademark to the Victor Talking Machine of Camden, New Jersey, which in 1929 was acquired by the Radio Corporation of America (Figure 6.4).

6.4 *RCA's Nipper*
Every industry has its lore, its folk heroes. Nipper has been a standard fixture for years.

When GE acquired RCA Inc. in 1986, it sold off Nipper along with the records division to West German's Bertelsmann A.G. publishing combine, which also owns Doubleday and Bantam Books. Although "Nipper" will now work for the Germans, who plan to retain the valuable RCA Victor name, he legally belongs to GE, which decided to retain copyright.

Today, there are an estimated 600,000 trademarks registered with the Patent & Trademark Office of the U.S. Department of Commerce. Of these, 55,162 were registered in 1986, and 54,500 trademarks were expected to be added to the books in 1987. Not included in these figures are the thousands of trademarks registered in the states where the products or services are sold, nor those registered in over 150 countries that are parties to the International Convention for the Protection of Industrial Property, first convened in Paris in 1883.

A common misconception is that the trademark is like a government license; in some countries, that may, in fact, be the case, but not in the United States, where the only way to establish the right to a trademark is *to use it*. By contrast, in such countries as Japan, the first *to apply* to register a trademark is often found to be the legal owner. Or exclusive rights may be granted to a trademark even though it won't be used.

Ronald McDonald knows. For nearly ten years, McDonald's Corp. was in the Japanese courts, arguing that Marushin Foods Company had ripped off its Golden Arches symbol simply by beating the Illinois company into the Japanese patent office by one day. It was clearly Marushin's intent to keep McDonald's out of Japan, but their lawyer, Mikako Fujiki, got the equivalent of a restraining order and spent the next decade turning it into a political hot potato. Meanwhile, McDonald's kept opening more and more outlets, so that by the time Marushin lost its case, McDonald's had its Golden Arches over 575 units—out of some 9,000 in 45 countries.

David S. Guttman, a Tokyo-based American patent and trademark lawyer, says "Any U.S. company trying to apply U.S. 'first use' principle is clearly leading with its left."

As if that weren't enough to worry about, foreign patent offices have been known to deny or reject registration to American companies whose trademarks are found to be "offensive or disrespectful" of local sensitivities. It is therefore quite unlikely that Borden Co. would ever try to foist Elsie the Cow on the more than 740 million Hindus of India, to whom cows are sacred animals.

Legally speaking

While a trademark is the same as a brand name, it should not be confused with a *trade name*, which identifies the business, not the product. Thus, while "The Eastman Kodak Company" cannot be registered, the word "Kodak" as part of the trademark can be, and is. Nor is a trademark the same as a copyright or a patent, which are applied for separately. Figure 6.5 illustrates the trademark, patent, and copyright elements of the Get'm!™mousetrap package.

The legal definition of a trademark is "a word, name, symbol, label, picture or device, or any combination of these, used by a merchant or manufacturer to identify his goods and to distinguish them from those made by his competitor."

Trademarks can be owned and/or registered by individuals, partnerships, corporations, or associations "or other collective groups."

There are four types of marks that can be federally registered:

1. *trademarks that identify products* (Kodak, Milky Way, Tylenol)
2. *service marks used in the sale or advertising of services* rather than products (Prudential's Rock of Gibraltar, Eastern Airlines' abstract falcon)

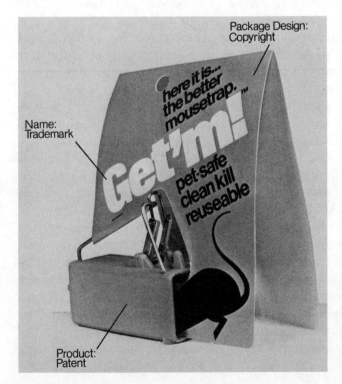

6.5 *Get'm! Mousetrap Trademarks* concern commercial origin identifications (they are marks of trade); *copyrights* concern literary and artistic expressions; *patents* concern functional and design inventions.

Brand Name & Package Design Credit: Selame Design

3. *collective marks* used by members of cooperatives, associations or other collective groups (AFL-CIO, the Teamster's wheel, the Woolmark, Cotton Council's tree)

4. *certification marks* showing the products to have been certified as to quality, manufacturing method, materials, etc., by a party (U.S. Department of Agriculture's "USDA-shield," Underwriters Laboratory's "UL-approved)."

Under the terms of the 1946 Lanham Trademark Act, which unified all the federal statutes and amendments enacted since 1870, one does not have to register a mark to use it. Nor does registration have to take place within a given time period, as the "first-use" clause of common law gives it some protection until such a time the applicant can show the mark to meet standards of registrability. Still, registering a trademark would be prudent.

For one, the act itself gives notice of the applicant's claim to the mark, thereby creating "presumption of ownership" and the exclusive right to use the mark, and forcing the other fellow to conduct a "due diligence" search. Secondly, the courts consider registration "conclusive evidence of the right to exclusive use."

Of course, no search is ever conclusive and most trademark attorneys will tell you that one can never be absolutely sure of being in the clear until, as one of them cynically puts it, "you've used a name or symbol and *haven't* been challenged."

Thomson & Thomson of Quincy, Massachusetts, one of the handful of trademark search firms (whose corporate identity we happened to design) says that of the nearly 1,300 searches it takes on each year, four or five of them produce "unwittingly duplicates."

"Next to patents, a trademark is probably one of the most valuable intangible assets that a company has," says T&T executive vice president Richard Harrington.

Private searches cost money while the government's doesn't. The trouble is that the Feds only have on file trademarks that are registered (only a small percentage are) and will only respond to any query with one name at a time, and not with a batch of sound-alike names.

U.S. trademark registration is good for 20 years and can be renewed every 20 years in perpetuity, provided that the mark is in use. Should a registered mark not be used, the courts have found non-use to be *prima facie* evidence of "abandonment." (There are exceptions to the rule: if a product is pulled off the market due to wartime shortages of material, corporate reorganization, bankruptcy, etc.)

After six years of non-use, the Trademark Office will cancel the registration. Under the law, it is also possible to engage in "defensive registration"—that is, to cover products not yet invented that may one day fit the company's marketing mix. Defensive registration is currently finding favor with those companies using invented or constructed names or proprietary symbols that are so familiar on certain goods that applying it to other goods might confuse consumers.

Companies entertaining the idea of getting a trademark can do what George Eastman did: go for one utilizing meaningless or arbitrary brand names. As noted in the previous chapter, Kodak is a meaningless name and, therefore, eminently protectable. An example of an arbitrary brand is Arrow for shirts, or Camel for cigarettes, because these names have nothing to do with the product and thus can be protected.

Arbitrary trademarks can also utilize numbers, initials, mythological or historical names, e.g., "Prince Albert" pipe tobacco. But unless picture-words are carefully chosen and designed to stand out from similar images—Indian chiefs and royal crowns, for example—the consumer is apt to be confused and remember the artistic device but not the company's name. (It is one reason we believe that wherever possible, for double protectability and memorability, that the picture mark be forged out of the organization's initials, e.g., IP (International Paper), Goodwill Industries, PBS (Public Broadcasting Service.)

A *suggestive brand name* is another option if the manufacturer wants to convey usage of the product. Not as protectable as the meaningless or arbitrary brand name, the suggestive mark is nevertheless quite effective. P&G's *Head & Shoulders* shampoo, for example, is clearly directed at dandruff sufferers: Nestle's *Decaf* needs no explanation nor does Gillette's *Dry Look* line of hair sprays and gels. AMF's *Heavyhands* is an aerobic exercise weight that, indeed, makes the hands heavier while jogging.

The third type to be considered is the descriptive mark, but it may be the most difficult to protect. It describes the product (Popsicle), is the name of the founder *(William Wrigley, Jr. Co.)* or is the name of the place where the product or service originates *(Wausau* Insurance). In order to protect such a mark, a second meaning in the minds of the public or competitors must be imparted (Figure 6.6). Without that second meaning, the mark might not qualify for registration. The best way of protecting a descriptive mark would, of course, be to employ a unique design.

Registration is ultimately the safest means of protecting your investment. Without it, the courts could favor challengers by finding such unprotected marks "generic"—in other words, up for grabs.

It happened in 1921 when Bayer lost its exclusive rights in the U.S. to the name "aspirin." In 1936, DuPont's "cellophane" became common property. Others who lost included Kellogg ("corn flakes"), General Motors ("frigidaire"), A.B. Dick ("mimeograph"), and King-Seely ("thermos").

To make sure it won't happen to them, companies such as Xerox, Coca-Cola, 3M and others frequently run institutional ads reminding the media to always

6.6 *Popsicle Ice Pops*
Example of a descriptive name, Popsicle, and line extension names, Creamsicle and Fudgsicle.

Package Design: Peterson & Blythe
Reprinted with the permission of Peterson & Blythe.

capitalize their brand names or indicate in other ways that they are branded products.

Another approach is to link the word brand to the name, as General Foods does in all of its advertising copy for "Sanka-brand" decaffeinated coffee or 3M for "Scotch-brand" tape.

Akio Morita remembers what it took Sony Corp. to protect its name (derived from coupling the Latin root for "sound" and the word "sunny" for optimism) from a rapacious Tokyo candymaker who registered Sony *Foods* after the electronics firm had become wildly successful.

But instead of suing under Japan's arcane trademark laws, Sony's lawyers sued for unfair competition. "In trying to prove the name was open for anyone to use," Morita writes in his memoirs, "their lawyers went to all the major libraries to show the name was in the public domain, but they were in for a shock. They came away empty-handed because . . . they could not find the word 'Sony.' We knew they would: we had ourselves discovered it long ago. The name is unique, and it is ours."[1]

It is even more important today. Sony, which used to have at least 18-

---

[1] Akio Morita, *Made in Japan: Akio Morita and Sony.*

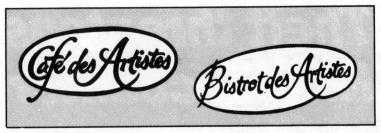

6.7 *Café des Artistes*

months' lead time before its rivals could catch up, now finds Matsushita and Toshiba so on top of things that Sony is in what Morita describes as "a parity situation." He says that when it is no longer possible to distinguish Sony from the rest of the crowd, "the only tools left are our name, package design and image creation."[2]*

In 1978, New York restauranteur George Lang discovered a goldmine on Manhattan's West Side: the Café des Artistes. The 60-year-old restaurant had fallen on bad days. Its leaded glass windows were shattered and the sensuous murals by Howard Chandler Christy had been papered and painted over by a succession of owners. Lang bought and spent a fortune on restoring it to its original splendor, and soon won over New York's finicky food critics.

Nine years later, the George Lang Corporation filed a $4-million trademark infringement suit against the Bistrot des Artistes *(sic)* of Cleveland Heights, Ohio. It charged owner Alton F. Doody with willfully misappropriating Lang's work, to the extent of copycatting the original's famous logo, even its nude murals—but not its cuisine. Lang only heard about it when customers called him to ask if he planned to open up *other* branches (Figure 6.7).

---

*So zealous is Sony in protecting its CI that since 1960 it has won numerous infringement suits against much smaller businesses that in no way could hurt its electronic sales. In one recent case, it is bearing down on a Baltimore fast foods/catering service called Sony's. It is the nickname of owner Resurreccion (Sony) Florendo, a Filipino. She tried to placate the lawyers by offering to rename her place "Sony Florendo's," but the lawyers aren't buying; they want assurances that upon her death her family won't use the Sony name. "That's too much," she told the *Wall Street Journal.* "I'm an immigrant in this country with no roots. All I brought with me was my dignity, my principles and my name. My parents gave me that, not Sony Corp."

---

[2]Morita, *op. cit.*

IT'S PARAMOUNT NOT TO TINKER WITH THE SYMBOL

When Gulf + Western acquired Paramount Pictures Corp. in 1966, it also bought a venerable corporate trademark that predated the studio's founding by two years.

After 52 years of continuous use, it was regarded as so familiar and enduring that the parent company left it alone: they simply added the legend, "A Gulf + Western Company."

Older than Leo the Lion and Columbia's torchbearer, the symbol, the trademark began as a doodle on the back of an envelope.

The artist was film distributor W. W. Hodkinson, whose Paramount Company was acquired in 1916 by film pioneers Adolph Zukor and Jesse Lasky and made the rental-distribution arm of their Famous Players studio.

Hodkinson had drawn the cloud-ringed mountain in 1914, from memory as a child growing up at the foot of Utah's Wasatch mountains. He "borrowed" the name from an apartment house under construction that he passed on his way to work.

The case is as yet undecided but the general test for trademark infringement under the Lanham Act is whether consumers are likely to be confused as to "source of origin of goods sold under the accused trademark."

Trademark infringement jury awards can run into the millions if the misappropriation is found to be willful. So can out-of-court settlements. In 1974, Goodyear Tire & Rubber spent $6.5 million to promote the "Big Foot" steel-belted radial tire, and another $6.2 million on an out-of-court settlement, unaware that Big O Tire Dealers Inc. already had a tire by that name. Sometimes the price of "theft of intellectual services" can be costly in other ways.

In 1976, RCA and its design consultants were publicly humiliated when station KUON-TV and the Nebraska Educational Television Network sued the NBC Television Network for misappropriating its red-white-and-blue *N* logo.

As the pioneer in color TV programs, NBC had been using a peacock to identify what was then called "colorcasts."

"We didn't consider it either a symbol or a trademark," recalls M. S. (Bud)

Rukeyser Jr., then NBC-TV vice president for public relations. "It was a promotional device."[3] The network still needed a logo.

The N designed for NBC by Lippincott & Margulies (which had earlier recast the identity for parent RCA) was no deliberate knock-off but an accident. But the Nebraska educational broadcasters didn't see it that way. After the new logo made its debut on the January 1976 Super Bowl game, NETV threatened suit.

"It was a PR disaster," says Bud Rukeyser, now NBC-TV Executive Vice President. "There was no way that anyone out in Nebraska might've confused one of our sitcoms as an educational show," but as NBC had "tied up substantial sums in developing the logo"—and more to the point, *wanted to keep it*—NBC settled.

Parent Company RCA gave Nebraska NETV "nearly $1 million" worth of used, state-of-the-art camera and studio equipment, plus six months of management services and "some cash."

By 1986, the NBC "N" had long faded from view, replaced by an updated version of their peacock, now *promoted* from a promotional on-air device to the network's corporate symbol, a stylish peacock (Figure 6.8).

---

[3]Personal interview of M. S. (Bud) Rukeyser, Jr. by F. Peter Model.

6.8 *NBC Peacock*
From top to bottom: The original peacock was abandoned in 1976 for an initial. A few years later, many missed the warmth of an organic element and brought back the bird to nestle within the N. A few years later, a totally new peacock above the initials NBC became the official symbol.

Latest Design Credit: Chermayeff & Geismar Associates

Trademark thieves

But no such legal redress awaits those trademark registrants whose "intellectual" property is willfully stolen as part of a massive counterfeiting program.

In 1984, Congressional action beefed up the law, making trademark counterfeiting a criminal offense, but the law is unenforceable outside of the United States. Merchants of such bogus goods are never jailed, and willingly accept fines as one of the hidden costs of doing illegal business.

So General Mills discovered a few years ago after the Izod Lacoste alligator began showing up on bogus "Lacoste" shirts manufactured in the Far East and sold off the back of trucks and by sidewalk "merchants" all over the U.S.

The Lacoste logo dates back to 1926, when French tennis pro René Lacoste launched his own line of 100% cotton sportswear. General Mills had purchased the license in the 1970s. By the late 1970s, the alligator logo was pulling in $596 million at retail.

The Lacoste scam represents only a droplet in the counterfeit bucket. According to the U.S. International Commerce Commission, bogus products are siphoning off close to $12 million a year from legitimate commerce, but the damage to General Mills's quality *image* was so devastating that its Crystal Brands division could never retrieve millions it had lost on account of canceled store orders due to "street traffic."

In 1985, it spun off Crystal Brands to its divisional management. Crystal has since recovered by taking on such winning lines as Ship 'n' Shore, Monet, Yves Saint-Laurent, and private label women's wear for Sears and Penney's. CEO Richard Kral hopes to revive Izod, remembers it "as more than a brand . . . a cult . . . almost a religion." He is convinced there's still life in the Izod alligator.

But Lisa Bernbach, co-editor of *The Preppy Handbook* (which had built the Izod "cult") isn't so sure. "Speaking for my fellow preppies, I'm not much interested any more with garments bearing alligator emblems."[4]

And speaking for Wall Street is Goldman, Sachs apparel industry analyst Jay Meltzer: "It's hard to become exclusive again once you've been nonexclusive."[5]

---

[4]Lisa Bernbach, "Can Kral Put Bite Into Crystal 'Gator?," *Crain's New York Business*, February 23, 1987.
[5]Phone interview of Jay J. Meltzer, Goldman Sachs, by F. Peter Model.

Making corporate symbols sing and dance

It takes no more than a passing glance at the parade of corporate ads and "tombstones" in today's newspaper and magazine business pages—or at weekend television's public affairs programs—to understand why most top managers no longer regard symbols or trademarks as mere "icing on the cake," but as the yeast that makes the cake rise.

What all effective corporate symbols have in common is that their owners and their design consultants met most or all the criteria governing good visual communication. Four stand out as critical, as all commercial symbols should always be:

- clear, not confusing; original, not imitative; functional, not frivolous; distinctive, not forgettable.
- meaningful, instantly conveying the purpose and personality of the corporation.
- easy to recognize, pleasing to the eye; have no unfavorable visual connotation in countries of registration.
- adaptable to advertising in all media and capable of serving as the unifier of a total identity program.

The following is less a criterion than an immutable law: *any symbol or trademark that requires more than a few seconds of thought to get its message across is not doing what it is supposed to do.* And that is to communicate the nature of the bearer's business or synthesize how it perceives or positions itself in the marketplace.

Superfluous as it may seem, an effective logo can become a better selling tool with a clever slogan. Apple Bank's advertising always includes the slogan, "We're good for you"—perhaps a subtle suggestion that a deposit a day keeps the bill-collector away.

Such slogans do more than "translate" abstract symbols; they enhance them. Thus, there are two good reasons why AT&T's symbol never appears without the legend, "The Right Choice." One of them is MCI, and other is US Sprint. Until January 1984, the consumer had no choice.

Actually, there's a third reason. In this age of creeping automation, as ATMs and other electronic gadgetry reduce the amount of person-to-person contact in transactional relations, business is keenly aware of the need to appear "user-friendly." Many corporations would like to project themselves as being members of the community who will lean over backwards to help their neighbors.

As we shall see later in this chapter, financial services organizations are becoming particularly symbol-oriented. And banks, freed from having to do only local business, are increasingly turning to symbols and slogans to reaffirm that they are still upstanding members of the community.

Sometimes it is difficult to live up to a slogan, as was the case with New York's Citibank's "The Citi Never Sleeps." Introduced to promote 24-hour banking-by-machine, it was found wanting after the bank was slow to repair its malfunctioning ATMs. Citi was quicker to repair the slogan to the empathetic "We're Thinking What You're Thinking."

The bank learned what many corporations are discovering—that a corporate slogan has to live up to its promise always if it is to be a positive asset to the identity.

Advertising often loses sight of its mission by allowing technique to override the message. Technique may win Clios,—advertising's version of the Oscars— but if you start out with a strong symbol, as Citibank does, and use it consistently and well—that symbol plus a realistic pithy tagline will do more to instill consumer confidence than any lengthy ad.

How does one go about selecting the right corporate symbol?

"Personal preferences, prejudices, and stereotypes often dictate what a logo looks like," says IBM design consultant Paul Rand, "but it is *needs*, not wants, *ideas*, not type styles, which determine what its form should be."[1]

The question is, "*Whose* needs? *Whose* ideas?"

Before the designer puts pen to paper, management has a number of important tasks to perform. The first is to convey a vision of where the organization is going, which involves a clear assessment of the corporation's strengths and weaknesses, what markets it will compete in, how it will compete, and the major programs now in the works and planned for the visible future.

Various design concepts and approaches are developed and shared with the client. A vital dialogue is necessary at this stage to produce new insights and further clarification in order to bring out *subjective* feelings about the various design options open to the client-consultant team.

At the end of this most important meeting, a clear picture of what direction the final design should take should emerge and *be agreed upon by all parties concerned.*

The decision can be equally as important as selecting a new name. For once a symbol undergoes implementation, its visual impact is apt to be far and wide and, given the corporation's investment, long-lasting.

Because the right symbol has the proven potential to profoundly influence corporate growth—internal as well as external—the designer or design team should be given as much access to the company's long-term strategic thinking as sound business practices will allow.

The designer brings to the table his or her creative skill, but unless and until that designer becomes very familiar with the various "faces" the company wants

---

[1] Paul Rand, New Name and Identity Announcement Brochure, Spring 1986.

to project (as well as those it would rather not) the designer will find it difficult to anticipate management's likes or expectations.

One of the first things Steven P. Jobs did after being ousted from Apple Computer—the company he co-founded with Steve Wozniak—and setting up his newest computer venture called NeXt, was to engage the counsel and design services of Paul Rand.

Rand is one of the grand old men of corporate identity. He has created many timeless images, including Westinghouse, UPS, and IBM, for which he is still design consultant.

Jobs insisted that Rand involve himself "totally" in the company's planning, participating in as many conferences and discussions as his busy schedule would allow.

Steve Jobs is an unusual entrepreneur in more ways than one. There are few start-up companies willing to commit $100,000 to finding a symbol before there is even a product to promote. Jobs could, because NeXT (Figure 7.1) was financed

7.1 *NeXT*
"Splitting the logo into two lines accomplishes several things: it startles the viewer and gives the word a new look, thus making it easier to separate from common usage. Even more importantly it increases the letter size two-fold within the framework of the cube. For small space, using a one-line logo would have been too small to fit within this same framework.

"Readability is hardly affected because the word is too simple to be misread. Moreover, people have become accustomed to this format with such familiar four-letter word combinations as: L O
                                    V E

"In its design, color arrangement, and orientation; the logo is a study in contrasts. Tipped at a jaunty angle it brims with the informality, friendliness, and spontaneity of a Christmas seal and the authority of a rubber stamp. Together with its lively, black silhouette, it becomes a focal point difficult for the eyes to avoid."—Paul Rand

Design Credit: Paul Rand

with $7 million of his own sizable fortune, plus the backing of Texas billionaire H. Ross Perot and two universities, Stanford and Carnegie-Mellon.

But more than that, Jobs is convinced that names and symbols are as much a part of any corporate culture as its product. He just proved it at Apple, especially with the Macintosh.

Jobs was hardly the first to prove that. As Creative Director of Advertising & Sales Promotion at CBS Television, the late William Golden used to tweak the brass with such pronouncements as "a trademark does not in itself constitute a corporate image, but it can serve as a reminder of a corporate image—*if you have one.*" They finally told him to get them one.

Golden, who died in 1959 at the young age of 48, had come up with an on-air service mark that would establish an identity for the fledgling CBS Television Network that was separate and distinct from that of CBS Radio.

In a posthumous collection of his work, Golden described it as "a still composite of several concentric eyes against a cloud formation. The camera dollied in to reveal the 'pupil' as an iris diaphragm shutter which clicked open to show the network identification (CBS) and clicked shut."

In time, the CBS "eye" *became* the corporate image—not just a promo for the TV network (akin to the early NBC use of the peacock) but the visual *persona* of the entire company.

Still, there are CEOs who don't quite understand why their presence is required at the christening of the new logo, or why they should have to ride roughshod on people within the organization who misuse it.

The symbol may be both artistic and artful but it should not be seen as "corporate art" anymore than the Frank Stella wall tapestry in the reception area is a "hanging rug."

"Corporate art," observes a Chase Manhattan aide to retired CEO David Rockefeller—like his late brother Nelson, a keen art collector—"is form over function. Our Chermayeff & Geismer logo is function over form. We use it on everything that moves, and doesn't move."

In industry, that's called amortization, making your investment pay for itself.

It should be no different in the realm of corporate identity: once the design investment is made, the company will want to use the symbol in whatever way it can, not just on letterheads, in ads, or on packaging.

For that reason, certain questions dealing with application must be asked near the start of the design/development cycle, not at the end. Here are the obvious ones:

• Will the logo be *flexible in a variety of applications?* How will it look on a variety of materials and surfaces—glass, plastic, chrome, brass, wood, kraft-

David J Linton
Director
Graphic Arts

Sun Company, Inc.
100 Matsonford Road
Radnor PA 19087
215 293 6974

7.2 *Sun Company*
From the smallest applications to the largest.

Design Credit: Anspach, Grossman, Portugal

board? Raised, embossed, embedded? Can it be used in TV commercials? In videotaping?

- Will the logo *reproduce well in many different sizes?* Will it be as effective in 1/4-inch size on an embossed business card, lapel pin, or tie tack as it is in 20-ft.-high letters on outdoor billboards? (Figure 7.2a, b) Sun card and tank)

- Will the logo enjoy a *harmonious shelf-life?* How will the symbol look when endlessly repeated, as on product after product on store shelves? Is it boring? Annoying? Trite? Or does it make you want to reach for the product?

- Will the logo *work well in print advertising?* Is it strong enough to stand out on a full-page black and white newspaper page, which often resembles a blur of lines, tones, type—and other ads? Is it as dramatic in black and white as in color?

"Less is more" still holds.

For high retention value, simple graphic forms are always preferable to complicated illustrations, because there are fewer lines for the eye to take in. The same applies to the design of symbols and marks, especially under today's varied and sometimes difficult viewing conditions. Symbols that cannot communicate in short exposures, poor lighting, and competitive surroundings are likely to be those that require viewer interpretations.

"Ideally, a logo should explain or suggest the business it symbolizes," says Paul Rand.[2] But this is not always possible, and not always plausible.

"A logo takes on meaning only if, over a period of time, it is linked to some product or service of a particular organization. What is essential is finding a meaningful device, some idea—preferably product-related—that reinforces the memorability of the company name."

Symbols come in a number of basic forms that can be expressed in a variety of shapes, colors, typefaces, and even textures (Figures 7.3, 7.4, 7.5, 7.6, 7.7, 7.8, 7.9, 7.10). They can be described as follows:

- *The Seal:* a name or group of words worked into one total form that are often recommended to and chosen by companies who might find it difficult to depict the scope of their business in a mark. It might also be appropriate for companies that want to use their names but against a background that will give the letters depth, warmth, and a design element that set them apart from all others. *Examples:* New York Life (Lippincott & Margulies, Inc.), Ford (corporate staff), Blue Seal (Selame Design), Kodak (Peter Oestereith).

---

[2]Rand, *op. cit.*

7.3 *The Seal:* A name or group of words rendered in a cohesive form. Designers: New York Life, Lippincott & Margulies, Inc.; Ford, Ford Staff; Blue Seal, Selame Design; Kodak, Peter Oestereith.

7.4 *The Monoseal:* A monogram or initial within a shape or seallike form. Designers: GE, GE Staff; PPG, Lippincott & Margulies, Inc; Westinghouse, Paul Rand; Volkswagen of America, Inc., VW Staff.

7.5 *The Monogram:* A letter or combination of letters rendered in a distinctive manner devoid of confinement. Designers: IBM, Paul Rand; TRW, Siegal & Gale; Thomson & Thomson, Selame Design; RCA, Lippincott & Margulies, Inc.

7.6 *The Signature:* A company name rendered in a particular and consistent manner. Designers: Eaton, Lippincott & Margulies, Inc; McKesson, Anspach, Grossman, Portugal; Ludlow, Selame Design.

7.7 *The Abstract:* A graphic device, geometric or otherwise, that represents a company or service. Designers: Atlantic Richfield, John Massey & Tomiko Miho; North American Rockwell, Bass/Yager; Chase Manhattan Bank, Chermayeff & Giesmar Assoc.; Chrysler, Lippincott & Margulies, Inc.

7.8 *The Glyph:* A pictograph that suggests a company's service or area of competence. Designers: United Fund, Base/Yager; Woolmark, Francesco Saroglia; Shell, Raymond Loewy; CBS, William Golden.

7.9 *The Alphaglyph:* A pictograph formed around a letter or letters that pictorializes a company's service or area of competence. Designers: Pinkerton's, Selame Design; International Paper, Lester Beall; Dana-Farber and Goodwill Industries, Selame Design.

7.10 *The Wordmark:* A signature which encompasses a glyph within the word. It combines two elements of identity into one. L'eggs, Roger Ferriter and Herb Lubalin; Thayer, Selame Design; Ditto Inc., Morton Goldsholl Design Associates.

- *The Monoseal:* comprised of initials worked into a form resembling a seal. The monoseal offers the same advantages as the monogram (below) but has the added benefits of being accented by the seal's background. The monoseal also satisfies those who feel that initials alone are too sterile. *Examples:* General Electric, Westinghouse (Paul Rand), PPG (Lippincott & Margulies, Inc.), Volkswagen of America, Inc. (Volkswagen AG Wolfsburg, W. Germany).

- *The Monogram:* here the initials are made to work in a unique manner, ideal for companies that are known by their initials. Such symbols also travel well multinationally, as long as the same alphabet is used in those markets. "There is nothing about the IBM symbol that suggests computers," Rand has pointed out, "except what the viewer reads into it." *Examples:* IBM (Paul Rand), TRW (Siegal & Gale), Thomson & Thomson (Selame Design), RCA (Lippincott & Margulies, Inc.).

- *The Signature:* a name rendered in a particular and consistent style, usually proprietary. Signatures are much preferred by companies that value their unique typestyle almost as much as their names. Some feel the advantage of the signature is that there are far fewer elements to worry about. *Examples:* Eaton (Lippincott & Margulies, Inc.), McKesson (Anspach Grossman Portugal), Ludlow (Selame Design).

- *The Abstract:* a geometric device. Abstract marks such as ARCO, Rockwell International, and Chrysler do not express gender or describe the nature of the company as well as the *glyph.* The intent of the abstract is not to be descriptive. Any visual connection to the company's product, services, or name will have to be established through promotion. *Examples:* Atlantic Richfield (John Massey, Carol Lipper & Tomoko Miho), North American Rockwell (Bass/Yager Associates), Chase Manhattan (Chermayeff & Geismar), Chrysler (Lippincott & Margulies, Inc.).

- *The Glyph:* comprised of simple graphic lines to tell a visual story about the company's name, major product lines, or area of business concern. Easy to learn, easier to recall, the wordless glyph is understandable all over the world. *Examples:* United Fund (Bass/Yaeger Associates), Woolmark (Francesco Saroglia), Shell Oil Company (Raymond Loewy), CBS (William Golden).

- *The Alphaglyph:* the simple graphic lines used to tell the glyph's story form an initial or set of initials. *Examples*: Pinkerton's (Selame Design), International Paper (Lester Beall), Dana-Farber Cancer Institute and Goodwill Industries (Selame Design).

- *The Wordmark:* A glyph combined with the signature as a singular whole that creates a more compact identity device. *Examples*: L'EGGS (Herb Lubalin, Roger Ferriter Agency), Thayer Pharmacy (Selame Design), Ditto (Morton Goldsholl Design, Associates).

NEW MAN

7.11 *NEW*
Designer: Didier Souloumiac; Art Director: Evert Endt; Agency: Raymond Loewy, France.

7.12 *Key Pharmaceuticals*
Design Credit: Selame Design

Also a possibility—but only for those companies with particular letters, that lend themselves to this sort of word-picture game—is the upsidon. Those of Key Pharmaceuticals and New Man show why (Figures 7.11 and 7.12).

Another possibility, a wordmark flowing into product initials, resolved an identity problem for the Army and Air Force Exchange Services (Figure 7.13).

When General John Long was assigned to head the United States' 11th largest retail organization, it was apparent to him that the retail operation nomenclature "Main Exchange" and "Mini-Mall" were not working to their advantage. "That's when I realized it was important that we obtain the services of corporate identity specialists," Long admits. "Selame Design recommended that we not reinvent the wheel; just get back to basics and legitimize the name we were born with over 90 years ago. The right name and visual image is very important; they instill pride. If they do nothing but give the employee pride in their organization, that pride will carry itself to the customer and inspire sales,"[3] explains General Long.

[3] Personal interview with General John Long by author.

7.13 *Army and Air Force Exchange Service*
Design Credit: Selame Design
The new retail store design system emphasizes the PX and BX in bold red, white and blue graphics and incorporates the AAFES identity.

This will be implemented in some 9000 stores around the world providing them with a familiar and consistant image.

®AAFES is a registered trademark of the Army and Air Force Exchange Service

7.14 *Number as Symbol*
Silver anniversary of New Seabury resort, Selame Design; Detroit's TV Channel 2, Selame Design; Prime Computer, Selame Design; 3M, Siegel and Gale; 4C's brand, Dixon Parcels.

The life span of a symbol

Theoretically, once selected and implemented, symbols should last forever, or at least until such a time as the logo no longer works, because the company that commissioned it merges, undergoes restructuring, or goes out of business.

In practice, symbols *do* change, either entirely (as in the case of AT&T, which was ordered by the court to rid itself of the familiar bell logo) or only cosmetically (as have the logos of Prudential, 3M, Westinghouse, Apple Computer, and many other firms). (See Figure 7.14.)

It is probably a good idea that dynamic corporations every so often step back to take a look at their visual presence and ask, "Is that symbol still really representative of us today?"

The AT&T case is truly unique. When AT&T settled its seven-year antitrust suit with the Justice Department in January 1982, it agreed to spin off its 22 local service phone companies. These then were restructured into seven regional holding companies, which would be restricted to provide only local service. It was allowed to keep its Long Lines network, Western Electric, Bell Laboratories, all of its equipment and all licensing rights to inventions developed at Bell Laboratories. Though effectively stripped of two-thirds of its assets, AT&T still thought of itself as "Ma Bell." Accordingly, it changed its name to American Bell and set out to build a new CI utilizing the bell symbol that had been designed in 1969 by Saul Bass (Figure 7.15).

But in June of 1983, just before American Bell got ready to unveil its new look, Judge Harold H. Greene enjoined it from using the bell symbol, ruling it had been part of the divestiture and so could only be used by the "Little Bells."

Stunned, management and Bass/Yager returned to the drawing board and in seven weeks came up with the current symbol and the monogrammed name of AT&T.

While it meets government standards, the new abstract globe is a symbol with no history, no pedigree, and thus tends to contradict advertising spokesman Cliff Robertson's reassuring "We've always been here when you needed us."

Another corporation that may be forced to change symbols soon is Procter & Gamble, although here the introduction of a new logo will be noticed less by consumers than by the trade.

In the early 1980s, a mysteriously flaky grass-roots letter campaign got under way, aimed at P&G's wholesalers, brokers, and store managers accusing P&G

1889   1900   1921

1939   1964   1969

7.15 Design Credit, 1969 Symbol: Bass/Yager

1.  This crude cross, painted by a wharf hand on a wooden box of Star brand candles around 1851, was the beginning of the "Moon and Stars."

2.  In time, the cross developed into this en-circled star—still merely part of the rivermen's ship-ping "sign language."

3.  The first standard trademark adopted by the Company was this roughly drawn crescent enclosing 13 stars.

4.  The 1882 model "Moon and Stars" had been refined to this point, and registered in the U.S. Patent Office.

5.  By 1902, our trademark, still basically the same, displayed some of the "gingerbread frills" typical of the turn-of-the-century.

6. Around 1920 the trademark became more simplistic—still, however, there was no fundamental change from the original design.

7. Finally, in 1930, a sculptor was commissioned by P&G to design today's authorized version of the famous "Moon and Stars."

7.16 *Procter & Gamble*

management of using its classic, 135-year-old "wizard/moon/stars" logo to subliminally promote "satanism" (Figure 7.16). By 1982, its corporate PR department had to respond to as many as 15,000 letters a month. The anti-P&G campaign has since subsided considerably.

Most companies would laugh off such a campaign as the work of a handful of malcontents or kooks, but not P&G.

The world's largest brand product marketer has always presented itself as squeaky-clean, family-oriented, and mainstream American. Up to 1986, it reportedly spent over $2 million to fight such an insidious crackpot campaign. Rather than continue to divert time and resources on continuing this forlorn battle, Procter & Gamble apparently has decided to come up with a new symbol.

Many companies hesitate to change their known symbols because they fear the result will be the loss of residual identity. Or, if they are retailers, they will worry about a consumer backlash. They really shouldn't. There will be some people who will take their business elsewhere because they correctly perceive the new identity signals other changes, but they are strictly in the minority.

A case in point: when Federated Department Stores sought to alter radically the image of New York's now-trendy Bloomingdale's from its old dowdy self in the early 1970s, it dropped the antiquarian signature for Massimo Vignelli's understated, lower-case logo. One shopper wrote, more in sorrow than in anger, that doing so depersonalized the old store (Figure 7.17):

"I can't help remembering the John Wanamaker signature which had so much class and could not be aped by anyone. As scribble and unsleek it may have been, but I believe what J. W. signed [just] as I believe what [book publisher] Alfred Knopf signed. Behind each signature stood the proprietor. But behind the sleek lettering is an art director looking at his hand mirror."

Perhaps. But "irate shopper" missed the point entirely. Dowdiness has no place in marketing today, which is why traditional emporia such as Philadelphia's Wanamaker's and Strawbridge & Clothier's, and Washington's Woodward & Lothrop and Garfinckel's have all been snapped up by merchandise-minded megamarketing companies that place a premium on modernity. (Knopf sold out years ago to Random House, which is now owned by mega-publisher Newhouse.)

Modernizing symbols does not always call for dramatic alterations. Consider the new General Electric symbol and its imperceptible change from the older emblem.

According to officials at its Fairfield, Connecticut, headquarters, GE undergoes periodic reviews of its company-wide graphics. After it swallowed RCA in 1986, the internal review took on special urgency.

Although RCA as a company ceased to exist as of December 31, 1987, GE decided to retain RCA's cyrillic monogram developed in the early 1970s by Lippincott and Margulies as a brand label on TV sets and VCRs. GE also decided to

bloomingdale's

7.17 *Bloomingdale's*
Design Credit: Massimo Vignelli

leave the illuminated giant RCA letters on the sides of 30 Rockefeller Plaza—its home since the Thirties.*

Yet, some within GE's hierarchy were discomfited by the sharp contrast between the sleek look of the RCA symbol and the admittedly antiquarian appearance of the GE logo. They argued for at least a radical stylistic change, but ultimately, were voted down. Research showed its memorability factor to be extraordinarily high. Accordingly, it has modified the old monogram—"desquiggled," as *Forbes* Magazine succinctly described it—to improve clarity and legibility without diminishing the trademark's high level of recognition.

---

*But should the NBC radio and TV networks vacate 30 Rockefeller Plaza when their leases expire in 1997 for new studios and offices on Manhattan's west side, as now seems likely, the letters will come down. Spokesmen for The Rockefeller Group Inc. (RGI) say they "no longer refer to it as 'The RCA Building' but as 30 Rockefeller Plaza."

A GE spokesperson explains, "In the past, several forms of the trademark were used, including the signature with the words 'General Electric' on either side of the monogram. This has been de-emphasized and the modified monogram will be the primary symbol from here on in."

More lay behind the desquiggling than met the eye. The fact that the company has formalized the informal—employees have been instructed never again to refer to their place of work as "General Electric"—signals a sea change for Thomas Edison's old electric company. As *Forbes* put it: "Like a riverboat gambler [GE] shuffled its corporate deck by getting rid of 232 businesses and product lines for $6.9 billion, and acquiring 338 for $11.1 billion." Already in insurance (Employers Reinsurance), stock brokerage (Kidder Peabody) and electronics (RCA), GE is definitely stalking other, similar big game. Not being known as an electric company will surely help.

The financial identity crisis

The burgeoning financial services field, to which we alluded earlier in this chapter, seems to be a hotbed of identity change. In 1985 and 1986, more than 570 banks and thrift institutions either changed their names and/or adopted new symbols.

This number does not include banks that have made cosmetic changes, simplifying their names and modernizing their logos. The 1986 Dun & Bradstreet *Million Dollar Directory* suggests there is still much to be done. It lists 860 banks whose names start with "First National Bank of . . . ", 235 with "People's" in their name, and 160 with "Citizens'."

Now that banks can operate nationally, the First Nationals may either have to find a new name to project their sense of cosmic importance, or just drop it. That's what The First National Bank of Boston did—it is now just plain Bank of Boston, with a streamlined, more visible graphic eagle.

There's another reason why symbols play such an important role in financial services advertising: they convey the image and the implied tradition of longevity and trustworthiness.

In an era of deregulation, the roles of banks, brokerage houses, and insurance companies have become blurred and almost as indistinctive as their basic product packages. Banks sell stocks and bonds; brokerage houses sell insurance; insurance companies act as banks. And in this commodity business, consumers no longer switch because they want to build up their collection of toasters but because they want to place their money with institutions in which they have confidence.

In 1985–86, *New York Times* advertising columnist Phil Dougherty reports, the country's twelve largest financial services companies—including Prudential-Bache, Shearson/American Express, Citicorp, Merrill Lynch—spent nearly $293

DON'T SPRAIN YOUR LIGATURE: A FEW WORDS ABOUT TYPE STYLES

Many symbols today are used in context with standard typefaces. Increasingly, clients seek proprietary typefaces that exist in no catalogue, and which are therefore more protectible as corporate assets.

A good example is the very distinctive typeface designed for *The New Yorker* magazine in the early 1920s by the late Rae Irvin. It is copyrighted, and attempts to improvise on "Irvin type" have been consistently challenged by the publication.

Another approach is to modify an existing typeface ever so slightly so that it is *perceived* as proprietary—as in the case of the late William Golden's adaptation of the distinguished Firmin Didot into what is now universally regarded as the "CBS typeface."

Sometimes it is not necessary to design or modify an entire alphanumerical system. By altering or clustering just a few letters into a ligature, as in the case of the "st" in Westinghouse or the "ch" in New York's ChemBank (née Chemical & Corn Exchange Bank & Trust) the corporate name is doubly protected.

---

million on institutional and product advertising. Not included in this figure is what they spend on "collaterial materials" and graphics.

In such a cluttered advertising environment, the symbol that reposes in the consumer's memory bank clearly adds an extra dimension. Consider the case of ITT Corporation's Hartford Insurance Group and its famous symbol, the stag.

Until 1981, when the Hartford switched to policy-specific ads, the most memorable thing about its TV commercials was the Hartford stag, patrolling empty city streets at night by peering into shuttered storefronts, protecting children boarding yellow school buses. The overall message was plain: the ever-vigilant Hartford Insurance Group is on duty round-the-clock, in places you wouldn't suspect.

But after the stag was sent to pasture, recalls John Daly, the underwriter's director of creative communications, the Hartford name slipped from memory: unaided awareness of the Hartford dropped from 14 percent to 7 percent. Yet, despite its absence, when prodded, consumers "still associated the stag with the Hartford," Daly says. "The animal conveys we are old and reliable."

Other old symbols that have undergone cosmetic change over the past few years are the Merrill Lynch bull and Prudential's rock. The latter, first designed in 1896, has undergone eight upgrades, each one rendering the famous profile in simpler, clearer, eye-catching lines. The most recent (1984) change, turned the rock into a more simplified graphic (Figure 7.18).

Merrill's bull only recently became the firm's official logo, having literally stepped out of the TV commercials that made him even more of a mascot than dear old Elsie the Borden Cow.

In the old days, the firm's long, unwieldy monicker—Merrill, Lynch, Pierce, Beane, Fenner, & Smith—earned it the not-too complimentary sobriquet, "We, The People." In 1969, it simplified its name and began running its bulls—*plural*. Merrill wanted America to know its brokers were, as the ads said, "a breed apart."

That worked well for ten years, but when the small investor was temporarily driven out of the game, Merrill stopped appealing to the investor herd instinct and began focusing on a narrower consumer spectrum: the inner-directed, self-motivated, upward-mobile investor. No one really knew it at the time, but those ads spawned the present-day corporate symbol. Instead of the herd, consumers now saw themselves—the *lone* bull weathering a storm in a cave, pawing through the proverbial haystack, weaving gingerly through the equally proverbial china shop, trotting down the empty canyon of Wall Street on Sunday morning. The

7.18 *Prudential*

Design Credit, 1984: Lee & Young

| 1896 | 1900s | 1920s | 1940s |

| 1950s | 1970s | 1977 | 1984 |

bull, which began as the broker, had been metamorphosed into the prudent investor.

According to a Merrill spokesman: "There was nothing wrong with being 'bullish on America,' but it didn't reflect who we were and what we were becoming—less a giant investment house and more of an innovative firm, dedicated to serving the private investor." (italics ours.)

Bringing back the bull has also increased consumer awareness of the giant financial services house by as much as 15 percent in the first year of its revival, says an executive at Merrill's ad agency.

Another updating, one also reflecting a great deal of ongoing restructuring is occurring in book publishing. Not only are old-line publishers becoming conglomerates in their own rights, but as they move into such new operational fields as video, their colophons—once regarded as mere bagatelles—take on new importance as marketing tools.

Simon & Schuster, founded in 1924, is now the publishing and information services arm of Gulf + Western Inc. and since 1982 has experienced explosive growth. It consists of six large publishing groups (trade, reference, higher education, school, professional, and international) that are responsible for a total of 40 different imprints under such names as Summit, Linden Press, Fireside, Touchstone, Poseidon, and Pocket Books.

To provide a common denominator, S&S took its best-known colophon— "The Sower" (after a 19th-century French painting by Jean-Francois Millet)—and elevated it from tradebook to corporate status. It has replaced the ampersand between the names Simon and Schuster (Figure 7.19).

"The Sower" appeared on S&S's first book, the *Crossword Puzzle Book*, as a symbol suggesting the spreading of knowledge. Over the years it has become

SIMON 🚶 SCHUSTER

The original Sower
1924

The Sower
~1941

The Sower
~1980

The Sower
1986

7.19 *Simon & Schuster*

1939   1943   1945   1962   1964   1977

POCKET
B O O K S

7.20 Pocket Books *Gertrude*
Design Credit: Milton Glaser

such a fixture that S&S even turned to self-parody, e.g., Kay Thompson's & Hillary Knight's *Eloise*, spreading cookie crumbs, or Charles Addams' fiendish brat, Puggsley, scattering carpet tacks. An art deco update in the 1930s was dropped after Pearl Harbor because it too closely resembled the Rising Sun symbol of Imperial Japan. Meanwhile, Pocket Books' famous Gertrude the Kangaroo, with book in pouch, for which Walt Disney Studios charged them $25 in 1939, has undergone no fewer than six modernizations (Figure 7.20).

Conclusion

In the final analysis, symbols and logos should be thought of as they were in antiquity—as hard-wax seals that could only be changed by shattering the die. That thought ought to keep restless ~~CEOs~~ *executives* from toying with the notion of "making a few minor adjustments." ~~(See Figure 7.21.)~~

The late William Golden of CBS recalled that after a few years of seeing his "eye" appear here, there and everywhere, he ran into CBS President Dr. Frank Stanton.

"I timidly suggested we abandon it and do something else, for in 'show biz' you are under constant temptation to change for the sake of change alone."

Aghast at the suggestion, Stanton—who had made his name as a top-flight market researcher—told Golden he was out of his mind. "Just when you're beginning to get bored with what you have done is probably the time it's beginning to be noticed by your audience."

—. *The Company Image*

GENERAL CINEMA'S PROJECTOR: IF IT AIN'T BROKE, WHY FIX IT?

Some symbols, like fine wines, seem to improve with age. In 1961, shortly after going public and changing its name from General Drive-In Corporation to General Cinema Corporation, the firm began thinking in terms of corporate identity.

GCC retained Selame Design to come up with a distinctive logotype that could be applied not only to the company's printed material but also as a motion picture "trailer."

The result was a symbol that uniquely formed a movie projector— illustrating once again that often functional simplicity is the best solution. Had the initials GCC been left horizontal, it would have ended up a stationary symbol; on film, it became a dramatic, moving sequence that, accompanied by a snare drum riff, announced the showing of that night's Feature Presentation.

Billion dollar cake

From 1964 to 1987, annual revenues soared. In December, 1987, GCC Executive Headquarters celebrated with a "Billion Dollar Cake." "It took 23 years to go from $16MM to 1 billion dollars and we expect to come close to doubling the billion in a year with our new acquisitions," is Richard A. Smith's optimistic attitude.

With 1,254 screens in 340 locations in 37 states and the District of Columbia, ticket and lobby concession sales still account for a substantial 35% of revenues. But growing even faster are GCC's non-cinema revenues, drawn from both product diversification and equity trading. These activities have required a symbolic deemphasis on the "movie business," since GCC is now also known on Wall Street as:

- The nation's largest independent bottler of Pepsi-Cola, as well as one of the largest bottlers of Dr. Pepper, 7-Up and Sunkist (a brand it created in 1978 but subsequently sold to RJR Nabisco, which also bought its 19% stake in Heublein).
- Holder of more than 59% equity in Neiman Marcus Group in Dallas, Bergdorf Goodman in New York and Contempo Casuals; as well as 18% of Great Britain's Cadbury-Schweppes PLC candy and soft drink concern.

7.21   *General Cinema Corporation*
In 1985, General Cinema Corporation felt the need to reevaluate its identity. They decided a subtle identity change would be in the company's best interest. The retention of identity equity became the challenge. The solution was to develop a new mark that flowed from the old, without the literal visual relationship to the projector.

GCC now is not only the largest theatre company but the largest Pepsi-Cola bottler as well as the owner of a group of retail specialty chain stores.

Design Credit: Selame Design

Over 23 years ago, President Richard A. Smith, now Chairman, looked for a way to communicate to four major publics: "Our employees, our stockholders, our patrons and the general public from which we draw our future employees, stockholders and patrons."

Little has changed, other than the numbers and, to a degree, the ratios of General Cinema's marketing mix.

Accordingly, updating the "old" logo could be achieved by simply modernizing an already elegantly simple solution. Or as Dick Smith put it, "We sought to retain our heritage as a theatre company and, at the same time, better reflect our current status as a multi-faceted, consumer-oriented growth company. Throughout the last 23 years, our symbol helped distinguish us from the crowd. We are considered a very forward-looking company in the eyes of people both in and outside of our industry; and in that sense, it was very helpful. I think a professional image helps attract employees, particularly young employees, who think of companies as a career place and tend to want to go with companies that have a forward-looking, growth image. And, I think, the first impression of a company is often its name and logo (Figure 7.21)."[4]

---

[4]Personal interview with Richard A. Smith, Chairman of the Board, General Cinema Corporation, by author.

The product is the *package,* not the product

Before people knew the meaning of the adjective "biodegradable," industrial designer Henry Dreyfuss was asked if he didn't agree that the banana was God's idea of a perfect package. He closed his eyes, thought for a minute, and shook his head vigorously. "No, God made no provisions for getting rid of the peel."

The perfect package, Dreyfuss countered, "would be one that consumes itself right away," like an ice-cream cone. "It displays the merchandise. It allows you to see, feel, smell and taste it. And it is happily disposed of by the time you are through with it."

And like all good manufactured packaging, the ice-cream cone has a particular shape, when filled, comes in a riot of colors, and has a visual identity that is uniquely its own. The only fault Dreyfuss could find with the ice-cream cone was its utter lack of flexibility, having been designed to hold only one kind of product.

Although he spent most of his professional life as an industrial designer— the "Touch Tone" phone being one of his lasting contributions to present-day society—Dreyfuss devoted many of his final years to getting his clients to understand the importance of packaging.

Packaging, he wrote in his seminal book, *Designing for People,* should serve as "a silent salesman, an unwritten advertisement, an unspoken radio and television commercial. . . . "

If Dreyfuss were alive today he might not recognize the marketplace. He was of a time when consumers still *asked* for products and store clerks would obligingly retrieve them. Self-service was in its infancy.

Today, the only "clerks" that exist work for law firms, and consumers are left to fend for themselves in stores that are often larger than the hangars that were built to house the early jumbo airplanes that Dreyfuss also designed. Moreover, shoppers are now regularly confronted by a staggering array of products. Theirs has become, as someone wisely put it, "a tyranny of choice."

Thus, when even the corner gas station has become self-serve, the package can no longer be regarded as the container that holds the product—but more often than not, it is seen as the product *itself.*

The package must also serve as a communications medium. As long as there were sales helpers, manufacturers saw little need to provide consumer information. Now, in order to protect consumers—often from themselves—federal regulations specify that food packages, for example, must display nutritional data in a specific location, as well as size or net weight, and a complete list of ingredients.

The package must sell itself from the minute the product is introduced. In many instances, the package may be the manufacturer's *only* sales tool. It asks to be picked up, to be considered. It is designed to intrigue, to arouse curiosity. It will even carry its own testimonials by "satisfied" users who may or may not be famous personalities.

The package doubles as an advertising medium. It is cheaper for a manufacturer to put all of its claims on the box rather than on the TV tube. Nobody "zaps" the box. In fact, the package as advertisement may be the manufacturer's last best hope for "reaching" shoppers. It is certainly the most cost-efficient way of reaching users since *the package is the only medium that keeps on delivering impressions long after it has moved from store to home.*

The package is also the "star" of its own TV commercial. Numerous advertising studies show that advertising that shows the package as it appears in the market or in use at home scores consistently higher recall than ads that merely describe the product or praise its virtues (Figures 8.1, 8.2, 8.3, 8.4).

Finally, the package has the ability to reduce operational costs. It not only conveys information to consumers, but also, when color-coded, it improves warehousing and distribution, and speeds its own delivery to the point-of-sale (Figures 8.5, 8.6).

Dreyfuss may have seen it coming. "The paradox of packaging," he observed, "is reached at the cosmetics counter where the vial is often more costly than its contents."

And for good reason: 83 percent of what we learn we learn by seeing, as compared to learning by tasting (1 percent), touching (1.5 percent), smelling (3.5 percent), and hearing (11 percent).

This being so, packaging's greatest impact is probably ephemeral. Dreyfuss sensed it by targeting cosmetics packaging: manufacturers are not just selling mundane products but *symbols.* And if, as the legendary David Ogilvy has often pointed out, advertising only works if it can convey a perceived benefit not readily apparent, then it is the package itself that serves as perhaps the single most important tool of modern marketing.

Certainly, it is that 83 percent figure that explains why, according to a number of reliable indices, the packaging industry has become the nation's largest industrial employer, and the third-largest in terms of sales.* In 1987, product packaging accounted for more than $50 billion in design, filling, plant operation, and allied services—roughly one-tenth of the value of all finished goods produced in America.

Packaging is a comparatively young industry, having emerged only at the end of the nineteenth century as a means of ensuring the safe delivery of breakable products from factory to customer. Prior to that time, people bought their comestibles in bulk and would bring their own bags, sacks, boxes, and containers for liquids to the store. Only a few merchants provided what we now call the "plain brown paper bag."

Post-World War I technology led to the development of laminated paperboard cartons, glass jars, seamless tin cans, waxed paperboard liquid containers; World War II technology gave us all sorts of packaging made of extruded plastic

---

*Not to be confused with other industries that "package" such nonconsumables as books, movies, plays, tax shelters, pension plans and political candidates.

8.1

8.2

8.3

8.4

8.1–8.4 *Kodak - Film Packaging*
In today's advertising, the package is often the star, so it should look the part. Reprinted Courtesy of Eastman Kodak.

Advertising Credit: McCann Erickson
Package Design Credit: Selame Design

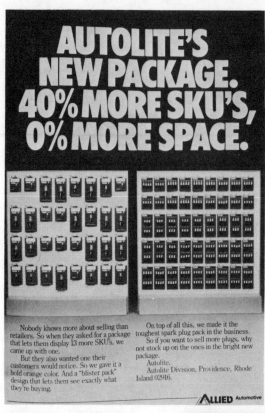

8.5–8.6 *Autolight/Fram*
When Allied's Fram and Autolight blister card products were repackaged to save paper costs and retailer space, they advertised this benefit to the trade.

Package Design Credit: Selame Design
Advertising Credit: Symon & Hillard

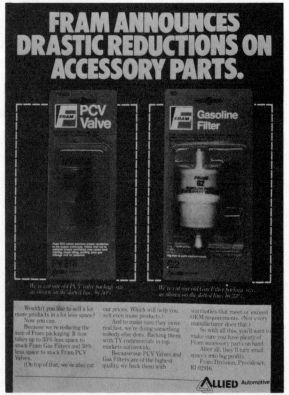

and polystyrenes. The Korean War left industry with a vast aluminum surplus and spawned the convenience dinner tray. Now we are into microwaveable and aseptic packaging of all kinds. Packaging's latest innovation—flexible, high-barrier plastics for perishable goods—is apt to have as great an impact on lifestyles as the tin can had at the beginning of the twentieth century.

Package *design* is an even younger industry, a by-product of *industrial* design that only happened to catch hold because of the Great Depression of the 1930s.

Hard times had crimped sales of many products that, at the time, were seen as *avant-garde* but that we now regard as utilitarian tools without which mankind would be lost—like the hand-operated can opener or pencil sharpener.

At first, recalled Dreyfuss in his 1955 book, "We would be called in to smooth out a few 'rough edges'" on the item about to be marketed. Literally. Squarish-looking appliances were made to appear rounder, "softer,"—and the market responded.

Hard goods manufacturers looked at the escalating sales figures and began to see the people were actually motivated to buy by the way things *looked.* Then industrial designers—Dreyfuss, Teague, Loewy, Nelson, Deskey, et al.—were asked to "look over the advertising" the agency had prepared. The package was still thought of as largely irrelevant.

In the late 1930s someone invented the supermarket, and eventually the package no longer seemed quite so irrelevant. It moved up there, with advertising. So did the industrial-*cum*-package designer.

To see how far we have come, a 1984 survey by Professor John Deighton of Dartmouth University's Amos Tuck Graduate School of Business found that 33 percent of corporations engaged in manufacturing products depend on outside design consultants. Only 16 percent still ask their advertising agencies to design their packaging.

The power of packaging

There is a reason for that—one that not only has to do with product movement but equally as important—to sustaining, even protecting, the established corporate identity.

A well thought out package design program, either as part of or apart from an across-the-board CI program, can rejuvenate an entire company by giving it a competitive edge it may have lacked. (See discussion of Sportcraft on page 145.) In the case of previously successful products that have been instantly made to look outmoded by the arrival of newer, more attractive rival brands, a packaging facelift can have an incalculable impact on the bottom line.

Invariably, such a packaging "rehab" program reverberates throughout the entire organization. Organizational pride, waning along with slipping sales, rebounds dramatically. Worker productivity seems to rise sharply, as often the product is seen as brand-new. And quite often a package facelift registers as well in the financial marketplace.

But the need for products to keep "looking good" is only one of many forces that keep the package designers busier today than at any other time in marketing history.

In addition to the flood of "newer and better" products (a subject we will address in more detail later in this chapter and in Chapter 9), today's manufacturer has other concerns directly affecting the organization's very survival as a viable player in what is often called "the cut-throat democracy" of the self-service marketplace.

- *Development* of newer, more innovative, effective, and economic packaging materials and methodology.
- *Invention and implementation* of new production, distribution, shipping, and warehousing procedures.
- *Enactment* of new, often tougher, federal, state, and local government regulations requiring extensive packaging changes.
- *Realignment* in market position due to shifts in consumer buying attitudes.

Understandably, the continuing and relentless pressure on manufacturers to develop new products with which to extend or protect existing lines imposes a heavy financial burden on most, regardless of the size of their business.

Yet, surprisingly, the cost of package design is actually the least important factor—to manufacturers as well as to the ultimate consumer.

It has been estimated that 75 percent of all finished goods are packaged in one way or another. Yet, taken overall, the cost to the consumer is surprisingly small—about 5 percent of each disposable dollar, and only slightly higher for foods and beverages.

Food products, because of their perishability, account for nearly half of all the money spent on packaging; the remaining 50 percent is split more or less evenly between pharmaceuticals, toiletries, cosmetics, household chemicals, and a staggering array of non-edible consumer and industrial products.

While it is fashionable to decry packaging as "wasteful," even the most vociferous of social critics recognize packaging to be essential for the preservation, distribution, and sales of retail, institutional, and industrial goods. They must surely recognize that were it not for packaging, the nation's food bill would cost at least $25 billion more.

Not only must the package be able to hold, stabilize, and discharge its contents with a minimum of fuss; it should be able to survive climatic extremes, be easy and safe to transport, discourage tampering and theft; attract, entice or intrigue the impulse shopper; provide product description, nutritional information, use-instructions and bar-coded price data for store scanners.

"Funds invested in creative graphic design and package research," notes John Deighton of Dartmouth's Amos Tuck Graduate School of Business, "will often yield a greater return than the same funds applied to media advertising—while accomplishing precisely the same goals of product awareness, image formation and incentive to purchase."[1]

In other words, packaging shouldn't be treated as the sizzle on the steak but as important to consumerism as the steak itself. Yet the shelves continue to groan under the weight of packaging that, upon closer examination, seems made of more fat than meat.

No full-blown university research is needed to show that many household product manufacturers still don't understand that all their advertising expenditures are meaningless unless the customer is motivated to *reach* for their package.

That's where smart design can make the difference. A technically flawed or poorly designed package that misrepresents the product within has a way of irritating shoppers into passing it by. Like the cannibals in Harry O'Neill's story, they no longer eat the missionaries; they ignore them.

In retailing, victories are measured in square inches of retained shelf and rack space. Accordingly, what is now taking place on the overcrowded shelves is nothing less than "economic Darwinism"—no winners or losers, merely survivors. Those viable products that do survive are likely to stand out in other ways.

To be sure, product quality matters greatly in shelf survival, since it is the repeat sale that guarantees longevity; but so does *perceived* product quality by first-time supermarket shelf reachers.

Consumers are always willing to try out new brands but they still instinctively select those bearing familiar manufacturers' names or symbols—Heinz, Campbell, Kodak, Hershey, Nabisco, etc.—over those they have never seen or heard of.

What all the top-selling brands in their classes have in common is packaging familiarity and continuity like that of Morton Salt (Figure 8.7).

What separates good package design from bad is the way the basic product message comes across. Presented in a visually and psychologically appealing manner to set the product apart from other, similar products, the message doesn't leave the consumer guessing. There is no marketing time for that. Most busy shoppers won't stop to remove the product and examine it closely.

Harvard Business Review editor Theodore Levitt observes that "people use

---

[1]Professor John Deighton, *A White Paper on the Packaging Industry*, December 1983.

8.7   *Morton Salt*

appearances to make judgments about realities. It matters little whether the products are high-priced or low-priced; whether they are technically complex or simple; whether the buyers are supremely sophisticated or just plain ignorant. Everybody always depends to some extent on external impressions."[2]

How a product is packaged is thus often more critical than what's inside. For it's the *package* consumers see, not the product, and it's the *package* that promises satisfaction to come.

The package is also the *last* message the manufacturer can send consumers as they stride past the shelf, their peripheral vision taking in at least 300 other package designs a minute. Yet, far too many manufacturers fail to realize just how

---

[2]Theodore Levitt, *The Marketing Imagination,* The Free Press, 1983, 1986.

crucial that split-second exposure can be to shoppers who arrive without a list—or the discipline to shop just for what they need.

"The package," insists former J. C. Penney head William (Mil) Batten, "is the last few inches of the thousand-mile pipeline linking manufacturer to vendor. It's those last few inches where the customer interfaces with the merchandise. If nothing happens here, the entire cost of getting the product to market is irretrievably lost. *Wasted.*"[3]

Netting the impulse shopper

Ten years ago, impulse buying decisions accounted for 65 percent of market basket shopping; put another way, only 35 percent of all brand purchases were planned before shoppers entered the store.

Today, says the Point of Purchase Advertising Institute (POPAI) of Fort Lee, New Jersey, impulse shopping generates more than 81 percent of cash register sales; planned shopping is now down to 19 percent.

And when the theme of a TV commercial is tied to an in-store display, or reflected in such other last-minute reminders as miniature ads mounted on shopping carts or in-store coupon give-aways, sales on particular lines can shoot up by as much as 500 percent.

What this means, simply, is that the mass marketers, who have huge co-op ad budgets and the ability to manipulate shelf space with all sorts of retailer-incentives, are no longer in control of their store environments. A former P&G brand manager, now a senior management official at Saatchi & Saatchi Compton Inc., remembers: "When we told them 'jump,' they asked 'How high?'"

These days, in a stunning role reversal, it's the manufacturer who jumps. Brand loyalties seem to be going the way of the 25-cent candy bar. Shoppers no longer regard leading brands as "status symbols." Instead they look for a product's *economy, convenience, and practicality.* As there are no clerks to direct their attention to any one brand, it's up to the package to convince the consumer of a product's worth.

A recent Roper Organization study bears this out. In seven product categories—tea, coffee, shampoo, beer, frozen orange juice, cola, and noncolas—Roper detected a sharp decline in brand loyalties. "We found *fewer* shoppers going into stores knowing what brands they wanted and *more* of them looking for brands that were 'best buys,'" says pollster Burns W. Roper. He attributes this in part to "more men shopping than ever before and advertisers still talking to women."

---

[3]Personal interview of William (Mil) Batten by author.

"This overwhelming shift of power to retailers," observes Keith M. Jones of Strategic Resource Group, a Connecticut market research firm, "has ushered in brand *hostaging*. Either a ransom is paid by the manufacturer in trade promotion dollars or his product will be denied in-store exposure."[4]

It has also led retailers to take a good hard look at private labels and store brands as a way to untie the last of their manufacturer's apron strings.

By upgrading the look, feel, and quality of their store brands, they win in three ways: restoring profitability to many marginal stores without necessarily harming nationally advertised brands, and using product to sell the store (image). It may even come to pass that in the supermarket of tomorrow, the store brand will be primary, while the nationally advertised brand becomes the "loss-leader" that brings in the customers.

All indications are there:

- Since 1968, there has been a 48 percent decline in the number of food stores—from 223,000 to 115,000. Fewer stores does not mean less clout, just more efficient operation as chains merge and consolidate and centralize their buying offices.

- The top ten chains now control 33 percent of national brand movement, and by the year 2000, they may control nearly 50 percent.

- By the year 2000, 85 percent of the stores will be scanner-based, capable of telling at an instant how well or badly a brand is doing, long before the manufacturers or wholesalers get around to doing their tallies and analyses of shopping trends.

- Private or store-brands are continuing to be formidable competitors to leading brands, especially when they present an upgraded appearance that reflects well on the corporate identity—as, for example, the Pathmark chain. In some chains, such as Jewel Tea's Star Markets in Boston, upgraded private label Star brands account for 33 percent of chain sales, proving that price-conscious shoppers do not need half a dozen brands in each category to fill their shopping carts.

- Although they peaked in 1982 when they accounted for as much as $2.8 billion in store purchases, "no-frill" products, are still costing brand-name manufacturers leverage by offering consumers plain-jane packaging, mainly in commodity products where shoppers detect little or no grade-differential.

- The recent emergence of "Price Club" members-only deep discount warehouse stores, which sell mainly manufacturers' overruns in bulk at 8 percent above wholesale, also attacks the very foundation of the Old Retail Order since many of the cased goods sold had been made for the *institutional* market, e.g., restaurant-sized Heinz ketchup jars.

---

[4]Keith M. Jones, *Ad Age*, April 27, 1987.

- The converse rise of the upscale supermarket that combines health foods, take-out delicatessen, bake shops, kitchenware, farm stands, and even home-service cooking—such as pricey J. Bildner & Sons and A&P's Food Emporiums in the Northeast U.S., and Gelson's in Los Angeles. Consumers are not willing to pay premium prices for staples but they are ready to spend for specialty foods that feature some of the most imaginary packaging going.

The shoe's obviously on the other fellow's foot. And it fits: consider how quickly manufacturers responded to retailer demands to come up with tamperproof packaging in the wake of the Tylenol scare—not just for drugs but for foods as well. Five years ago the response would have been lukewarm, with manufacturers insisting that the pipelines first had to be cleared of inventory. Now it's the manufacturers who clear out the inventory for the retailers. And voluntarily.

SOMETHING OLD/SOMETHING NEW

"Less" packaging and "more" product show-through gave two sports equipment clients another crack at a recreational health market that was itself in transition when we got involved.

For New Jersey-based General Sportcraft Co., the problem was how to reassert brand identity dissipated over 15 years of benign packaging neglect; for AMF American, the athletic division of what used to be American Machine & Foundry before its restructuring and acquisition by a Minneapolis conglomerate, the problem was how to reestablish credibility on a shoestring budget after several lacklustre seasons.

In 1981, General Sportcraft, a medium-sized packager of equipment for amateur tennis, volleyball, croquet, bocce, and badminton enthusiasts, saw to its dismay that it had become a commodity house. Instead of selling its products to large discount chains, catalog showrooms, and mass merchants—"the guys who bought in volume and stayed bought if the products moved," explains founder Ken Edelson, his company was haggling over price points with small sporting goods retailers. They also had a real problem: Pacman had lured indoors many of their backyard athletes.[5]

Compounding Edelson's problem: General Sportcraft equipment was quality stuff, but its packaging said something else.

Fifteen years earlier, in 1966, the company had undergone a complete package design program, but over the years, too many product managers had ignored the design system by tinkering with packaging, and by 1981

---

[5]Personal interview of Ken Edelson by author.

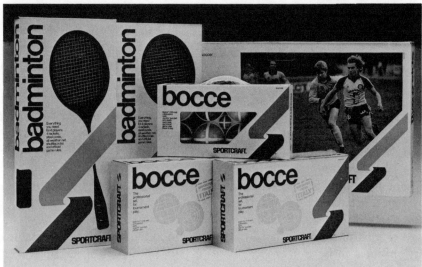

8.8–8.9 *Sportcraft*
General Sportcraft's old line of packaging appeared dated, without an overall, professional looking identity. Although they carried top-line professional sporting goods, many consumers failed to perceive this.

Design Credit: Selame Design

the line had lost all consistency and cohesiveness, and buyers were turned off.

Edelson was tempted to do the economical thing: to return to the 1966 standards and this time enforce them. But that would have dated the line, so he began anew. He proposed to let the consumer see, perhaps even feel, the products without opening the box, using see-through "windows," and to make the packaging represent the quality of the product (Figures 8.8, 8.9).

The family-of-products approach encouraged retailers to give Sport-craft products more display room, and as a line approach was something to which any buyer could respond, General Sportcraft within 3–4 years had more than doubled its business. "I thought it would take much longer," says a still-elated Edelson.

Matt Dingman's problem was different. The former AMF/American marketing manager was given only a total of $200,000 with which to launch not just a new product but a concept: small dumbbells that would give joggers upper body conditioning. The product was aptly named *Heavyhands*, and seemed certain to appeal to the Yuppies.

But the budget would buy little advertising, and Dingman knew that trends are not built on the floor of discount stores. It needed a certain pizzazz and upscale class that would appeal to stores like Abercrombie & Fitch and Bloomie's.

8.10 *Heavyhands*
Design Credit: Selame Design

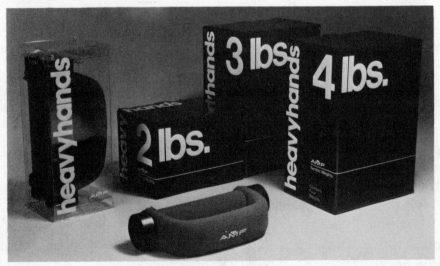

As the metal grips came wrapped in a sweat-absorbent bright red foam, we thought of putting *Heavyhands* into an "invisible" or see-through PVC box like the ones used by florists for orchid corsages. That would surely invite curious joggers to ask for in-store demonstrations. To complement the see-through box, the optional 2, 3, and 4 lb. weights were put in shiny black opaque boxes.

Together, see-through and opaque packaging made for an intriguing up-scale floor display and as Dingman says, "played a pivotal part in boosting sales from an anticipated $1 million to $10 million for the first year." *Heavyhands* also proved to be the hottest new fitness item during the 1983 Christmas buying season (Figure 8.10).

An even bigger threat to the old "pecking order" now comes from within: to retain precious shelf-space and build family groupings, a lot of new product is coming to market that in earlier days might not have even been considered. Indeed, it's starting to look like New Product Overkill, but this time, the victims may be the manufacturers themselves.

It has been estimated that each week, another 30 or so new products are introduced, and store management is getting to be hard-nosed about what it will accept for testing.

In just five years—1982 to 1987—there has been close to a 50 percent industry-wide increase in new product introductions. In 1986, the average supermarket stocked 16,719 lines while in 1987, according to *Dorman's New Products News,* the figure was up to 19,857.

"In 1987," reports Martin Friedman, editor of the monthly newsletter, "a record 10,182 new products were introduced—26 percent more than in 1985." Over 1,866 of these were food products, the rest, health and beauty aids, household and paper products, tobacco, etc."[6]

Most won't make it. Friedman thinks the 1987 mortality rate may run as high as 80 percent. This means that fewer than eight out of every 100 new products introduced in 1987 will be around in 1988 (Figure 8.11).

Richard Ponte, Vice President, merchandise procurement, of the Stop & Shop Companies in Boston, remembers that in 1985, "our grocery buying group was shown over 2,400 new products of which they accepted only 43 percent. Within weeks, they dropped 412 for lack of movement." Ponte points out "It's not just the new products, but the proliferation of what we call 'like-products.'"[7]

---

[6]Martin Friedman, editor, Gorman Publishing Company.
[7]Richard Ponte, speech to National Food Processors Association, January 1987.

8.11 *Safety 1st*
One new product in 1986 was so successful that it spawned other new and rejuvenated products, creating a children's safety accessories company.

This new product, originally brought to market as an unpackaged novelty, was repositioned through package design and new product identity; it was protected for future line extensions through a new corporate umbrella "Safety 1st." Baby On Board was an immediate success and became the launching pad for more than seventeen new products introduced in 1986.

Design Credit: Robert A. Selame

He cites "At least seven variations of Coca-Cola and three versions of Tide detergent in seven sizes." To get stores to carry the full line will mean that someone else will have to give up shelf space. The scanners will make that decision for managers.

With the power of product shelf-life or death slipping into the hands, as it were, of the robots, packaging assumes an even greater importance. For now, a new weapon has been brought to bear in the retailing wars: a *family* of products.

It is called "line-extension" and it was invented by manufacturers as a way to give them a better shot at retaining precious shelf facings or rack space. To maintain the family, no manufacturer can afford to have one or two more members systematically knocked off.

And now the makers of these products are putting their prestige on the line by placing the full weight of their corporate identities behind each product. Just a few years ago, who made what wasn't all that important: the product either sold or it didn't.

The new approach makes sense. At a time when a single 60-second TV spot can run as high as a million dollars, manufacturers are forced into making all sorts of end runs to get more bang for the buck. One such approach is the introduction of new products that can be tailgated onto established, older products of a similar genre.

Manufacturers can achieve their goals more economically through better package design—simpler, starker, more visible packages that clearly establish linkage in the mind of the consumer, at home, or in the store.

In 1982, with more than 40,000 products bearing the Kodak brand name, Eastman Kodak embarked on a still-ongoing program of unifying the appearance of its diverse packages.

Former marketing communications director Glenn Brown remembers, "It was hard to tell which of our products were sold where. It was hard to tell apart slide film from print film. The consumer was confused."[8]

Increasingly, so were retailers. For nearly 40 years, there seemed to be room on their shelves for only one kind of film: Kodak's. Its single unifying factor was the yellow box, but that was negated by a seemingly endless welter of unconnected symbols, insignia, code numbers and uncoordinated nomenclature. With various divisions doing their own ordering, it was not surprising that sometimes even the color yellow lacked consistency.

The necessity for change was thrust upon Kodak by a foreign pincer-movement onto its turf: from West Germany came Agfa-Gevaert's orange-boxed film, while from Japan came Fuji's green-boxed film.

And as if this weren't enough, there was the unanticipated appearance of "private label" film—good cloned stock made not by some fly-by-night suppliers but by establishment firms like Konica and 3M.

Their arrival meshed nicely with the emergence of such film-processing chains as Fotomat and their regional, even local, counterparts. Here, as in supermarkets, wars are won by price points. They would carry Kodak, of course, but they also took in the clones as "house brands"—in Kodak-*like* yellow boxes.

Fred Bonilla, a retail sales executive with Spiratone, a large New York mail-order photo supplier, explains: "Camera film has assumed commodity status. Yes, there is a discernible difference between the Kodaks and the clones but only to the professional eye."

"But the professional market is not what this battle is all about. If the retailer can make a few more cents—and few camera owners buy just one roll at a time—why shouldn't they? Kodak can't rest on its laurels anymore."[9]

They haven't. "In order to give our new 1000 speed film a demanding presence, we redesigned our familiar yellow box into a more protectable design," says

[8]Glenn O. Brown, Speech, *Ad Age* "Creative Workshop," 1983.
[9]Personal interview of Fred Bonilla by F. Peter Model.

Bill Loveland, of Marketing Communications. "Our design consultants (Selame) created the stylized K with a linear flow, and a bolder, cleaner typeface that capitalized on the equity of our corporate symbol. It's clearly a *family* of products now."[10]

Glenn Brown adds, "Despite the millions spent on television and print advertising, the strongest sales 'person' is still the package (Figure 8.12)."

Another strong advocate of the package as advertising medium is David F. Rowse, President of New England Apple Products Co. of Littleton, Massachusetts.

New England Apple was long on ambition but short on the kind of resources a Duffy-Mott, Welch, or Ocean Spray might pour into a branded product program. But by using a CI-oriented packaging program, Rowse's company not only "went national" in less than a dozen years, but moved from $7 million to over $100 million sales volume.

Established in 1856 as a small cider mill whose only other product was vinegar, nature's way of covering the founder's overproduction of apple cider in season, New England Apple Products was, until 1975, a low-margin wholesaler specializing in private label apple-based juice, cider, sauce and other commodities. Its sole retail label, "Veryfine," contributed so little to overall sales that some within the closely held company regarded it almost as a distraction—a family heirloom of great sentimental value, but little else.

8.12 *Kodak Family of Packaged Products*

Design Credit: Selame Design

---

[10]Personal interview of Bill Loveland by author.

8.13

8.14

8.15

8.13–8.17   *Veryfine*
Design Credit: Selame Design

8.16

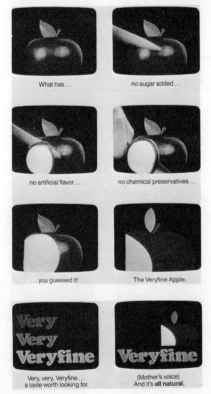

8.17

Yet it was *Veryfine* that helped Rowse achieve his goal of transforming the company into a sizable player in the back-to-basics food trade, then just getting started.

Veryfine's identity was nonexistent, lost in a sea of look-alike products. Our solution was to separate the product through the eyes: a strong graphic apple with a white slice against a black field, with a controlled system of usage for maximum retention.

"We put it on everything that moved out of here," recalls Rowse, "bottles, cans, corrugated shipping cartons, our trucks, brochures, billing forms, etc."

It worked so well because the identity system had a built-in plus: other graphic pictographs of fruit could be "plugged in" for line *extension*.

By the time Veryfine came out with its mixed fruit juice cocktails, consumers had become so accustomed to seeing the apple symbol many were not even aware of the switch to an orange, or grapefruit, or even a papaya, until it was pointed out to them. Talk about "memorability."

"By developing for us a distinctive brand identity," says Rowse, "our designers took a ho-hum generic product and made it into a nationally recognized brand. Unique packaging, subliminal labeling, coupled with a quality process [Rowse's patented 1957 system for extracting juice from Mackintosh apples], is the secret behind our stratospheric growth rate."

But mostly, Rowse credits the packaging (Figures 8.13, 8.14, 8.15, 8.16, 8.17)

HAVE PACKAGE, WILL TRAVEL:

When Holland's N. V. Philips' Gloeilampenfabrieken—which means "Mr. Philips' lightbulb factory" in Dutch—bought the Westinghouse bulb business in 1983, it set a very ambitious goal for itself: taking on GE, which enjoyed near-monopoly status in U.S. lightbulb sales, with a name well-known in 60 countries but not to American consumers.

"When you say 'Philips' in the U.S. people think it is spelled with two l's and is in the oil business," observes CEO Cornelis J. Van der Klugt.

Philips (which operates in the U.S. under the Norelco name) could not do with Westinghouse bulbs what it had done with earlier brand acquisitions, Magnavox, Philco, and Sylvania—which was to continue the brand. Part of Philips' acquisition deal with GTE called for retaining these valuable names for an undisclosed period of time to ensure continuity. But unlike Magnavox, Philco, and Sylvania, Westinghouse wasn't just a brand but a very big and viable industrial giant that is also in the broadcasting business.

Philips briefly considered using the Norelco name but thought better of it. Norelco was not just too closely identified in the consumer's mind

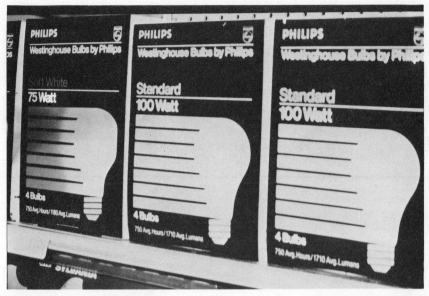

8.18 North American Philips
Design Credit: Kollberg & Johnson

with rotary shavers but was actually a corporate anomaly: it was set up in May 1940 as a trust by Philips to ensure that its U.S. assets would not fall into Nazi hands. The trust was dissolved only in December 1986, with ownership reverting to Philips, which may now choose to discontinue the Norelco name—meaningless elsewhere in the world.

To take on GE and also pave the way for its compact disc players, N. V. Philips spent over $20 million the first year—much of it in packaging. It is attacking GE with a pincer movement, advertising not just Philips bulbs but also Sylvania bulbs. The latter will probably be folded into Philips in the second year (Figure 8.18).

According to Philips' industrial design director Robert Blaich, CI and systemized package design are now regarded as "strategic elements" of the company's global marketing program. Centralized control resides at company headquarters in Eindhoven, Holland, but that, too, has to be fine-tuned.

Blaich recalls, "We had a Magnavox radio manufactured for us in Singapore but relied on Magnavox's advertising agency to design the package. The only trouble was that they had hired a designer who lived in Idaho. "All of a sudden, we got a frantic call from our man in the Taiwan assembly plant. The packaging was in the wrong languages for the wrong countries."

Blaich went to top management and successfully pleaded to put into effect a universal packaging system that would rely almost entirely on color coding and visual symbols—"a circle, square or whatever—anything that would not require any reading skills on the part of the native packers."

He got it. But then the real world intruded once again. The color code assigned to Asia turned out to be the color symbolizing "death" in Hong Kong.

"I suppose there must be exceptions to every rule," sighs Blaich.[11]

---

[11]Personal interview of Robert Blaich by author.

9

Brand identity: industrial, institutional, consumer

Brand identity is the *sine qua non*, the be-all and end-all of package design.

Clients need brand identity for their products to stand out in the crowd. Consumers depend on it as a quick and convenient guide to help them make the right choice at the point-of-purchase: if they are familiar with the product, it has a brand identity to which they can relate. Brand X, right alongside, does not, and it is likely to be passed up.

Industrial and institutional purchasers are also guided by brand identity, but the realization among those who sell to them is slower to sink in.

Quality (brand) images do not come about accidentally. They are created by design. Like all images, they tend to be relatively fragile. They must be continually nurtured, kept in shape, and constantly modernized in a rapidly changing world. Images can be depended upon to make the first or even second sale. After that, it's up to the product to live up to the image that has been created and propagated. The new products graveyard is cluttered with product images that failed to survive the consumer taste-test.

Industrial manufacturers have only recently come around to this belief. So have purveyors of institutional foods, a $200 billion sub-industry that, up until a few years ago, reportedly was growing at a rate three times faster than supermarketing.

For the most part these products are sent to market along with the barest necessities—drab, unappetizing packaging, and unattractive industrial-style advertising that might be more suitable for selling fuel-efficient ovens.

Until recently, the industry's overall approach could have been charitably described as studied indifference bordering on contempt for the end user—the very opposite tack food purveyors take in the consumer market. Interestingly, sometimes these wildly contradictory messages emanate from the same food companies. It may not be all that coincidental.

For years the institutional food industry was dominated by small, high-volume, low-profile processors and packers who saw no need for identity just as long as they earned their contracts through the bid system. They couldn't care less about "image," and could not be convinced to spend any more than was absolutely necessary on packaging. When asked why, their managers would invariably point out that since most of their end-users were low-skilled kitchen helpers who did not speak English, any expenditures along these lines would be wasteful.

They could not be more wrong: what is truly wasteful is food packaging devoid of handling and storage information.

We believe that good package design with bold color and a downplay of complex copy expedites kitchen handling by unskilled laborers, and over twenty years ago proved the point to a client, Goren Foods. The color-coding system for Goren's operates on two levels. First, it helps warehousing deal with an ever-growing product array, speeds inventory control, and simplifies the order-distribution process—all on the wholesaler level. Second, it clearly distinguishes Goren's traditional output of uncooked frozen meats from its precooked convenience line of meat entrées.

People react more quickly to color than to words. Traffic lights are color-coded rather than word-coded for this reason. It doesn't take long for a user to become thoroughly familiar with the product a color represents. Once he or she is familiar with the system, the person who must handle the product—whether in a warehouse or an institutional kitchen—can identify the product far more quickly.

Goren's added Spanish and other languages to the packaging since many of the kitchen employees in New York and other major cities come from the immigrant community.

Only in the past few years have other companies realized that those kitchen workers who can't speak English may be able to read Spanish. As a result, many packages now carry bilingual instructions. More of them even employ color coding.

Regrettably, too many institutional food industry executives still operate under the mistaken belief that "no one sees us" and that their disposable packaging, which goes from warehouse-to-walk-in-refrigerators-to-kitchens only serve as containers. They still do not understand that even institutional packaging can and should communicate and, yes, even sell (Figure 9.1).

"Institutional buyers," observes trade magazine publisher Don Karas of *Restaurant Business*, "are just as susceptible to products and services that convey a quality image as supermarket shoppers."[1]

The institutional food business is big, equal to about 40 percent of supermarket volume. It is an industry in flux. "The industry is fast being taken over by the very large food companies," says Karas. "The contraction reshaping consumer foods is now spilling over to here. These big suppliers—Nestlé, Campbell's, General Foods—don't play games. They're not shy when it comes to putting on a good show in packaging or sales presentations."[2]

The quaint notion that somehow purchasing agents march to the sound of different drummers than do ordinary mortals, that they are not influenced by appealing visual appeals but are only swayed by price points, is also being reexamined in the industrial products sector.

For more than 30 years, Olivetti, Herman Miller, IBM, Cummins Engine, and similar industrial pace-setters have shown the business world that attractive packaging and industrial design can sell more product (Figure 9.2).

IBM was one of the first to discover that it could make a professional image statement not only with its large mainframe and typewriter shipping cartons but

---

[1]Personal interview of Don Karas by F. Peter Model.
[2]*Ibid.*

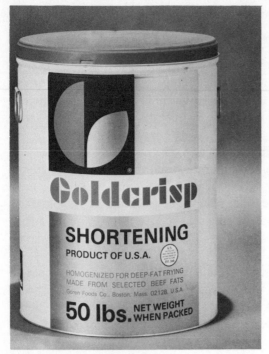 

9.1 *Goldcrisp Shortening*

Symbol and Package Design: Selame Design

also with its packaging for small lot office supplies. Every IBM ribbon comes in its own package and no opportunity is missed to sell IBM right down to the time the ribbon is installed (Figures 9.3, 9.4).

In markets where there is little genuine product differential, many industrial concerns have found it's better to put their money into packaging than advertising.

The modern industrial package must often be more versatile than its consumer counterpart. In addition to protecting contents that are often more fragile, such as microchips, the package also has to stack well and communicate the product's style, color and use through coding and nomenclature that is easy to see and understand in a variety of languages.

Since the creation of industrial products often involves an immense financial commitment on the part of the manufacturer, such packaging helps protect market position and fend off competitive assaults.

In smaller industrial companies such as Watts Fluid Power Company of Kittery, Maine, corporate and product identity are virtually inseparable.

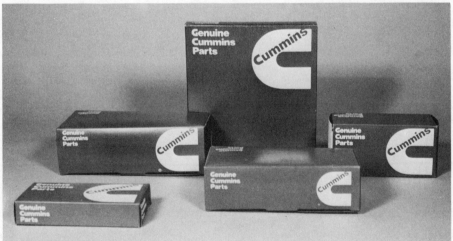

9.2 *Cummins*

Cummins, world leader in design and manufacturing of diesel engines, recognized the need for a new identity in 1973 and retained designer Paul Rand. The new company trademark incorporates the Cummins signature within the initial letter "C." This was then incorporated into every visual administrative and operating facet of the corporation. In his acceptance speech at AIGA's Fourth Annual Design Leadership Award, Cummins' Chairman J. Irwin Miller said, "A business is clearly best conducted if it seeks to do the best it can in every single one of its activities, great and small, neglecting none. If the businessman says, 'I care about how my products work, but I don't care about how my office layout works,' or 'I don't care how my stationery looks,' then he has decided to settle for less than the best, and this permeates his life. . . . Good design helps to form, in any one part of the business, an influence that affects all parts of the business. Good design, therefore, is very good business indeed!"

Symbol Design: Paul Rand

9.3, 9.4 *IBM*
Symbol Design: Paul Rand

Watts is the country's second-largest seller of air compressors, and at the time we entered the picture, was selling its two main product lines mainly through distributors. It wanted to sell direct to new markets. It wasn't properly dressed to do so, however.

We suggested that they change their name (not a big change) to Watts Fluidair Inc., a protectable name that would represent its true business concern. We totally revamped Watts' visuals so that its CI as well as its product literature conveyed a feeling of swift moving air, precision, and innovation. Years later Watts Fluidair Inc. is a totally different company from the one we visited in 1980.

Now that the consumer marketplace seems to be exploding in many directions—with food stores selling automotive products, gasoline stations dispensing convenience foods, drug stores stocking beach apparel along with tanning lotion, loveable Snoopy selling ice cream, etc.—the old order of "retail classifications" has changed materially.

And as market delineations become increasingly blurred and practically indistinguishable, more and more attention is being paid to the task of sustaining and protecting brand identity.

In the consumer soft goods market, as in upscale food stores, the manufacturer's brand is now under direct assault by a new and unexpected challenger, the store or "private label." Unlike the private label of past years, this one's got teeth: it's the *quality* private label and some are on the verge of achieving promotable brand status.

Private label coming of age

Traditionally, in the packaged goods industry, there are four ways of developing private label identity: *generic, rubber-stamped, endorsed,* and *proprietary.* All but the first have proved profitable (Figure 9.5).

- *Generic:* here the objective is to add "no-frills" product more as a public relations gesture to customers on fixed incomes or government assistance allowances (food stamps). The package carries no store or brand identification, makes minimal use of color, utilizes cheaper packaging materials, and works best in the product categories of household cleansers, paper products, and condiments (Figure 9.6).
- *Rubber-Stamp:* in this, the most cost-effective of all four, the identical corporate name, symbol, typestyle and color is used on all products. A skilled user of this approach is Pathmark.

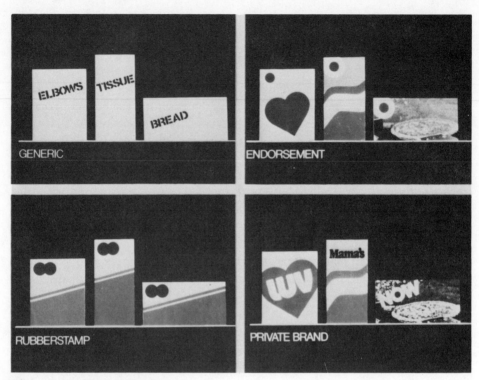

9.5 *Generic & Brand Identity*
Four possible approaches for private brand labeling.

Pathmark is convinced that using unified branding in both name and graphic design in its supermarkets, drugstores, and gas stations allows an exchange of equities among various products and product lines. They seem not be to worried about any possible confusion in the consumer's mind between Pathmark cake mix and Pathmark detergent, since the company presumes its customers are (a) looking for economy, (b) sufficiently literate to read labels, and (c) recognize and appreciate Pathmark's reputation for quality (Figure 9.7).

- *Endorsement:* here the retailer's name and identity are highlighted in a prominent position, but packaging design, color, and graphics vary depending on product category. Because different colors and graphics must be used to meet categorical marketing objectives, this approach may cost more than the rubberstamp (Figures 9.8, 9.9).

- *Proprietary:* in this approach, private label lines are developed as branded products, each with its own visual identity, but giving little or no indication of true ownership. The idea here, of course, is to give a national brand image to a retailer's products. Two of the most successful practitioners are Sears Roebuck, with

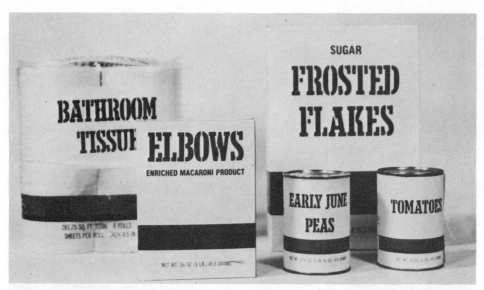

9.6 *Generic Identity*
Large black type indicates contents of package with no visible store or brand identification.

9.7 *Pathmark*

Symbol Design: Lippincott & Margulies, Inc.

9.8 *Abercrombie & Fitch*
Abercrombie & Fitch Redux: To bid for the upscale market, Oshman's—Texas-based mass market sporting goods company—purchased the name of defunct New York sportsmen's store and is developing brand image around a safari symbol of the rhinoceros. Using rubber-stamp approach, rhino identifies everything from food to clothing and accessories.

Symbol Design: Selame Design

its "Kenmore" lines of large and small appliances, and J. C. Penney, 80 percent of whose merchandise is private label.

"Just because it's 'private label' doesn't mean the product has to look cheap," says an official of New Jersey's Supermarket General Corporation, operator of more than 137 Pathmark stores.

Pathmark is not just in supermarkets, but also in drugstores and gas stations. And private labeling is not only being done in foods but also housewares, hardware, clothing, and even computers.

Outside the supermarket, private labeling becomes a far more complex—and controversial—subject. Especially when it involves wearing apparel.

"Private label as it exists today isn't what it used to be," says Max Garelick, senior vice president and general merchandise manager for the BATUS Retail Group (Saks Fifth Avenue, Marshall Fields, etc.). "It used to be just knock-offs and the most basic items."[3]

---

[3]Max Garelick, *New York Times*, 1986.

9.8 *(continued)*

9.9 *Kroger*
Design Credit: Lipson, Alport, Glass and Assoc.

Today, when retailers like Garelick talk about store brands, they do not think downscale but *upscale*. There is certainly nothing dowdy about the J. C. Penney dresses designed by Halston or the apparel that mega-model Cheryl Tiegs promotes for Sears under her name.

Department stores are in the forefront of the store label movement. They no longer feel the need to impose their names over their suppliers' names. They know that to insist would be to stretch consumer credulity.

"Today," says an editor of *Women's Wear Daily*, the so-called Bible of the rag trade, "everyone who's into fashion recognizes that big retailers do not own or operate their own clothing factories in Taiwan or Hong Kong. They also realize that one can find the same styles in different stores made by the same outfit, sometimes within days of the Paris previews, and that one or two outfits make them all."

Not for nothing has the circulation of Fairchild's "W"—the weekly version

9.10 *Proprietary Identity*
Product groupings, differentiated by a number
of names and a variety of package designs; suggests that the retailer carries a wider choice of
branded goods than does the rubber-stamp
approach.

of *Women's Wear Daily*—climbed to a circulation of 227,600 "civilian" readers.
There are few secrets left in or even outside today's apparel world.

To the buyers at Dayton-Hudson "private label" means their Boundary
Waters; to their counterparts at Filene's, it means the British Allen Solly label,
now under exclusive license here in the U.S. to the Federated chain. Neiman-
Marcus, Broadway and Bergdorf Goodman have since 1984 increased their "store
label" volume from $25 million to over $200 million.

The realization that everyone—not just the economically disadvantaged—
appreciates a bargain and that an "enhanced" private label program can generate
better profits than name brands, hit retailers in the late 1970s.

It started in the supermarkets 20 years earlier, when the major brand marketers began packing store brands as a mutual accommodation: they would give
the low-margin store merchant a few more cents markup while giving the producer additional shelf facings without its competitors being any the wiser.
Although at first there was little if any difference in product packed, the concept
began to pale even before it started to boomerang.

The extra inches of shelf space earned by the giant food and household products marketers with their proxy brands cost them sales—in effect, damaged their
own, carefully nurtured brand images. After all, if Brand X was really comparable
to the leading brand, why buy the more expensive product?

And since secrets don't last very long in any business, supermarketing as well as Seventh Avenue, word quickly got around concerning who was making what for whom. Soon, the majors began turning down private label jobs, driving retailers into the hands of other, less quality-minded suppliers.

It didn't take long for discerning shoppers to tell the difference between nationally advertised brands and Brand X—and to reach only for private label products where quality doesn't matter so much: household cleansers, paper products, pasta, kitchen salt, sugar, flour, etc. In time, it paved the way for generics, which first came into being during the 1979 recession as a PR ploy by Chicago's Jewel Tea, and then spread like wildfire until 1982, when generics began to slip.

It can't be stressed enough to say that private labeling was a *retailer-driven* movement based on hard-nosed economics. The manufacturer didn't need it, still doesn't need it, unless it is—as they charitably say—a "marginal" business that needs all the orders it can process. It is still the seller who convinces the maker that there is more than one way of splitting the retail dollar, that it really doesn't "cost [manufacturers] all that much more" to run the production line another hour.

To reiterate, if private label brands are treated like stepchildren, over the long haul brand identity will always win out in the end.

At first, external appearances may seem insignificant. What matters is *price.* As long as the price is right—meaning if it can be counted on to move product without benefit of costly advertising or P-O-P appeals—a deal can be made. And when packaging does come up for discussion, as it does more often these days, the talk was less frequently how close one can come to cloning the leading advertised brand without being sued. Today, smart retailers use private labels to establish their own brand identities. "The battle between manufacturer and private brands has taken a new turn." says Professor Walter J. Salmon of the Harvard Business School.[4]

Manufacturers are opening up their own high-quality specialty retail stores—either as self-contained units inside department stores or outside or both. Two good examples: Ralph Lauren's Polo and Laura Ashley.

An even better example is San Francisco-based Esprit De Corp. Founded in 1979, Esprit used to sell its branded sportswear in as many as 2,400 retail shops. Now it's down to under 1,000, having meanwhile opened up 30 of its own "super-stores" and expecting to franchise another 40 a year. Its 1986 sales topped $800 million.

Esprit's success is no fluke, but the result of the meticulous—some even say "fanatic"—attention founder Doug Tompkins pays to the smallest visual detail.

---

[4]Walter J. Salmon and Karen Cmar, "Private Labels are Back in Fashion", *Harvard Business Review,* May/June 1987.

Interviewed as one of five up-and-coming young tycoons on the PBS series, *Entrepreneurs,* Tompkins admitted to being "uncompromising" when it comes to protecting Esprit's product identity and store image.

The brand identity is everything. "What do you think all that advertising that we're putting out is for? It's for name brand identification!"

Tompkins can be a scourge even to his wife Suzanne, who also happens to be his business partner. On the PBS show, he recalls lacing into her on a shoe-buying expedition to Brazil because, when he asked about the Esprit labels in the shoes they had just ordered, she casually replied, "Oh, we'll put them on afterwards."

Upon hearing that, he says he became a madman, screaming at her in public that the label had to be as much a part of the shoe design as the sole or threads, that the label should always be on "top of the product spec sheet, never the bottom!" He says he has little faith in retailers. "If you wait for them to help you [promote], forget it. Who'll do the best image job with our product? Not them. Nobody will or can do it better than us!"

The feeling seems to be reciprocal. Retailers will grit their teeth whenever Tompkins shows up. "The Tompkinses are the toughest vendors, the worst s.o.b.'s in the market," complains one top store buyer, "but I'd never drop them." One retail giant that will not have to worry about the Tompkinses dropping in anytime in the forseeable future is J. C. Penney.

Unlike Sears, which maintains a financial interest in many of its vendors, J. C. Penney has traditionally kept loose rein on its estimated 10,000 vendors. Until recently, that is. In the *New York Times* in April 1987, a story announced Penney's signing a letter of intent to purchase 20 percent of a San Diego sportswear supplier of junior clothes. For the $18.7 million investment, Beeba's will "work with Penney to create junior speciality shops in about 100 Penney stores in early 1988. Free-standing stores are also being planned, the company said. Beeba's will be the main source of merchandise for the shops."

But this historic lack of control is now cited as having directly created some of the identity problems that in 1968 led J. C. Penney to undertake its very ambitious corporate identity overhaul—a program that reached into every nook and cranny of the company.

The company was founded in 1902 as a frontier outpost by James Cash Penney, the Bible-thumping 27-year-old son of an itinerant Baptist preacher. Penney lived by slogans. "Live Better for Less" was his favorite. And until the day he died, in 1971, at the age of 95, the company he built that became the world's third-largest mass merchandiser (after Sears and Kresge's K-Mart) seldom wavered from its founding principles. The words "style" and "fashion" were seldom spoken in Mr. Penney's presence.

It was, admits retired board chairman William Batten, "as if our image had been frozen in an earlier, simpler, innocent time."[5]

While Sears leaned to rock-and-roll with evolving consumer tastes and product performances, J. C. Penney stuck to its comfortable two-step. It would not desert its blue-collar, lower-middle-class, thrifty, all-American family customer.

In 1957, Batten—who was then assistant to Penney president A. W. Hughes—drafted a 150-page merchandising "white paper" that, for the first time, confronted the Board of Directors with the questions: What sort of company does Penney's expect to be in 1968? In 1978?

Batten proposed that the company begin narrowing its mass appeal by upgrading quality, prices, and styling and adding household products, even hard goods.

The Board vacillated, but assented to a line expansion.

Divisional managers responded enthusiastically. They began laying in new products with abandon, making their own deals left and right. In the absence of a company policy on private labeling (let alone store graphics and standardized packaging), Penney's over the following decade added as many as 300 store labels. Many were sold only to mail order customers, ostensibly to cut costs; it turned out to cost more than anyone had bargained for.

In 1963, K-Mart began its locust-like march across America, and it galvanized the Board into letting Batten—now chief operating officer—open up the first J. C. Penney "full-line" store. It stocked 70 percent soft goods, 30 percent hard goods (appliances, furniture, carpeting, sports equipment, even auto supplies). Over the next six years, Batten added 200 more "full-line" units, closing hundreds of "soft-line" stores. He was on a proverbial roll: 60 percent of Penney's 1969 profits came out of the former.

Two years earlier—in 1967—Batten had recruited Ed Gorman as marketing assistant. He would prove instrumental in getting his boss to think about systematizing packaging and store design. "Ed forced me to make the commitment to image and identity," Mil Batten says today. "And part of that commitment was to spend whatever it took to get the job done."

Batten, Gorman, and others interviewed twelve design firms. They narrowed the list to five, and settled on Unimark, a Chicago firm (now defunct) to do a four-month long, $20,000 audit of Penney's existing CI.

"What they really came back with," says Batten, "was the proof that the JCP logo was dreadful and that we had far too many brand names that meant nothing to our customers."[6]

Robert Smith, who had, in the interim, been hired as design manager with a mandate to try and sort out all these products, remembers having "to get out a chart before I could figure out which store label stood for what product."[7]

---

[5]Personal interview of William (Mil) Batten by author.
[6]Ibid.
[7]Personal interview of Robert Smith by author.

His people pruned 300 labels down to 85, and then to 48—still too many.

Although regular Penney customers had become accustomed to the house brands they regularly shopped, an in-house poll revealed to management that to a majority of Penney customers, the brand name didn't matter.

"Only a handful had equity," says Smith today. "One of them, 'Big Mac,' had the highest recognition of any man's work-clothing brand in the United States—yet too many of our shoppers identified it as a *Sears* brand!"[8]

Meanwhile, Unimark was hired full-time and over the next two years targeted fifteen different visual communications media, including store architecture, interiors, advertising, product design, and eight major categories of packaging.

Having clearly established that its future lay with young, more affluent consumers, J. C. Penney dropped products and lines that did not enhance its projected image. Out went the automotive centers (sold to Firestone Tire & Rubber), as did the appliances, outdoor lawn products, and no fewer than 45 private labels. "Would you hit the slopes on J. C. Penney skis?" Batten asks, rhetorically. Skis were seen as products of which the young, upscale customer would know more than Penney's sales staff. Likewise for diamonds, VCRs, and cameras. "None would be successful as J. C. Penney products," Batten says.[9]

Gradually, over 24 months, the new Penney's visual identity system emerged and was phased in quietly so as to allow existing letterhead and packaging supplies to be used up. It would take three years for the Helvetica-based CI signature to become ubiquitous.

Store modernization took place during the slow summer selling season; many stores were shut as new ones were being added at the rate of 50 a year.

Batten now says, "The design program saved the company from obsolescence. If we hadn't altered the image, it's conceivable Penney's would be where W. T. Grant is today."[10]

(Grant's folded in 1975, the biggest bankruptcy in U.S. retailing history, with $1.2 billion worth of merchandise sold off over a five-week auction that netted creditors 50 cents on the dollar.)

---

[8]*Ibid.*
[9]Batten, *op. cit.*
[10]Batten, *ibid.*

10

Design environment: where planning really pays off

This is the story of the most famous highway sign in American history.

In the summer of 1951, 38-year-old Memphis real estate developer Kemmons Wilson packed his wife and five children into the family car and headed off on vacation to Washington, D.C.

Along the way they stayed in a succession of seedy roadside motels, one tackier than the next. What particularly galled Wilson was having to pay $2 extra for each child. "It made my Scotch blood boil," he liked to tell friends.

After returning to Tennessee, convinced that what America needed was a clean, moderately priced, family-oriented motor hotel, Wilson by 1953 had opened four Holiday Inns, one astride each of the main roads leading into Memphis.

Three years later, Congress authorized construction of a 41,000-mile Interstate Highway System, and the rest is lodging history.

"I put into Holiday Inns what I like, and I think the public will like what I like," Wilson would tell everyone. He made air conditioners, wall-to-wall carpeting, modern Danish furniture, icecube dispensers, swimming pools, TV sets in each room and accommodations for children at no extra charge standard features.

Holiday Inns, as everyone now knows, was a runaway success. The company became a conglomerate, and went international. By 1987, Holiday Corp. had grown to become the world's largest hotel chain—1,600 Holiday Inns in 53 countries, plus 200 or so niche-operations such as the upscale Crowne Plazas, budget-priced Hampton Inns, all-suite Embassy Suites, extended-stay Residence Inns, and Harrah's casinos.

"Great sign" = great growth

Flamboyant Kemmons Wilson, had little use for consultants, trusted only his instincts, and, having owned theatres before becoming a home-builder, had a flair for showmanship and a keen appreciation of what the movie trade calls "marquee value."

In the 1950s and well into the 1960s, more than 95 percent of Holiday Inn business was spur-of-the-moment "walk-ins." For that reason, in the beginning Wilson insisted on the gaudiest traffic-builders he could think of at the time — those 43-foot-tall green, yellow and orange neon signs, with their flashing arrows and blazing stars atop movie house marquees welcoming guests or saluting the local Jaycees.

In the late 1960s the more visually literate population took exception to garish signs in their cities and towns. For a few years, the battle to keep their identification signs was strong, However, by the late 1970s the writing was on the wall (or sign) so to speak.

But Holiday Inn couldn't admit their signs were environmentally offensive, so in looking for an excuse to dismantle the "Great Signs," they cited statistics showing over 97 percent of bookings were by reservation. In other words, no more "drive-ins" meant no more need for screaming signs.

This was easier said than done. To its dismay, the new management, after Wilson's departure in 1979, was told by market researchers that while the signs had a lot of things going *against* them—energy inefficiency for one, "an overall impression of clutter, confusion and inconsistent brandmark usage" for another—they *still* had enormous guest-luring residual time and had built familiarity into them. To scrap them would be unwise.

By way of compromise, the signs were sharply "downsized" to less than half their original size and "contemporized." The riot of colors—green, yellow, orange, pink, blue, red and white—that had been used in various ways was made a "proprietary" green, brighter and more vivid than the variety of greens used before. The script logo was made more legible and now would appear only in white. The starburst was scrapped in favor of an orange and yellow graphic element, a pinwheel-like symbol giving the illusion of a seven-pointed star.

And so as not to break with convention, the design consultants retained the movie-house marquee but subdued it considerably by banishing such traditionally corny messages as "Kilroy Was Here. Why Don't You Stop, Too?"

By the time Holiday Inns completes the world-wide changeover in signs, it will probably spend over $35 million—one of the largest and costliest visual identity overhauls in recent history—though in terms of actual installations, not as ambitious as those of such global oil empires as Exxon and Mobil (Figures 10.1, 10.2).

One might argue, in hindsight, that had Kemmons Wilson gone to a design firm instead of a local Memphis sign-maker for his prototype, it might not have been necessary to be spending all those millions. One might also ask whether, at any time, Wilson expressed any environmental concerns—but the question would have to be rhetorical. In the 1950s and the 1960s—indeed, not until the publication of Peter Blake's pictorial polemic, *God's Own Junkyard: The Planned Deterioration of America's Landscape*—such questions simply were never raised.

It is a question that, alas, even now, not enough clients ask of their design consultants or, for that matter, themselves. That they don't helps explain the visual pollution that is all around us. It not only offends the public but also has a backlash effect.

Blake, now Dean of Architecture at Catholic University, had first raised the subject of commercial land and cityscape despoliation in a 1961 *Horizon* magazine article. Encouraged by such New Frontiersmen as Interior Secretary Stewart L. Udall, he expanded his thesis into a muckraking book. It was such a devastating indictment of the outdoor advertising, tract housing, highway, oil, and fast

10.1, 10.2 *Holiday Inn old & new*
Design Credit: S&O Consultants

foods industries that *Junkyard* became the *J'Accuse* of the early environmental movement.

Within a year, Lady Bird Johnson had joined Blake et al. at the barricades, and Congress passed the 1965 Highway Beautification Act. Since then, the number of outdoor billboards has dropped more than 54 percent to a 1987 base of 500,000.

But the real problem was not only the outdoor advertising industry but the

permanent exterior signs for the fast-growing roadside industries—service stations, convenience stores, fast food shops, etc.—that seemed to sprout willy-nilly whenever a new road was put down or an old one widened. Many units had been acquired as stronger chains swallowed up weaker ones, and little attempt was made to bring the latter into architectural line. Even less regard was being paid to how they might blend into the local scenery.

Business and government have only recently become aware that their joint environmental responsibilities do not stop at the polluted water's edge but also take in *visual* environmentalism.

A new corporate consciousness of planned and intelligently applied visual design in on the rise. It would be naive to attribute it all to the spirit of good corporate citizenship. Much of it is rooted in commercial self-interest—the realization that you don't have to shout or scream to get noticed. The better your visual statement, the more welcome-carpets will be rolled out for you.

As a direct result of rampant overcommercialization over the past 20-odd years, federal, state, and municipal governments here and abroad have enacted many restrictive ordinances covering architecture and signage.

Each week, new statutes are added to the books. While they clearly create major design and production problems for clients and consultants, they ought not be roundly condemned as limiting commerce but praised for liberating it. They are forcing all of us to take stock of our natural, visual resources, to unclutter the landscape while enhancing people-to-people communications.

That is, after all, what image and identity are all about.

Whether your organization is in the private or public sector, its activities industrial, manufacturing, retailing, institutional, financial and other services, perhaps the single most important decision that management will ever have to make is environmental: *where and how to display the newly developed visual identity.*

In this chapter and the next we will examine the question of how to apply the corporate identity in areas other than product, packaging, and on paper — *environmental* application. As with any environmental question, there are two sides: the pragmatic and the ideal—the commercial and the social.

Once you leave the immediate perimeter of self-interest and tread into "the public interest", sector, client responsibility takes on a new, different, and often challenging meaning.

It is one thing to place your new CI on a shipping carton that eventually gets mulched and recycled, or on a TV commercial that fades from memory as fast as it fades from view. It is quite another matter to paint it on a huge gas storage tank next to the New Jersey Turnpike where it will be observed for years on end by millions of motorists.

Clearly, once the decision is made to "go public" with an identity, parochial and commercial needs are transcended and a greater common good must also be considered and respected. Any organizations using the outdoor environment have a moral obligation to see to it that their imprint will not add to the visual pollution that already characterizes so much of the urban and exurban landscape. They should also view this obligation as self-serving: visual imagery that seems out of place is as bad publicity as that which is out of control.

Are your signs and buildings assets or detriments to the asthestic quality of the environment? In short, will you be welcomed or rejected by the local zoning board?

The first and second oldest forms of communications are the symbol and the word. The third is a combination of the first two: the sign.

Signage (or signing) serves to convey essential information in as few words as possible, and in our busy lives, even a few words may be too many. Hence, the evolution of glyphs and their wide application in airports and rail terminals worldwide. We know that people in a hurry do not stop to read: instead they react visually and decide viscerally.

America is a nation of signs. It is also one whose entire economy is built on advertising. By now, it is clear that visual identity—regardless of how or where it is conveyed—can be a cost-effective supplement to, and, in many instances, an alternative to high-priced and short-sighted advertising. Such "free" promotion— a misnomer, of course—is going to be a great deal more visible, to more people and for a longer time span than any paid media ad (Figures 10.3, 10.4).

Consider a story that appeared in the April 27, 1987 *Crain's New York Business* about the residential moving business in a city where 17 percent of the population (7 million households) moves every year. It is a business shared by no fewer than 225 companies—many of them local franchisees of such heavily advertised chains as Bekins, North American, Mayflower, Allied, etc.

"Moishe Mana, a 30-year old entrepreneur, has shaken up New York's residential moving business. . . . In just three years, he has become [the city's] second largest, carrying as many as 12,000 households a month. *Getting his 18 red moving trucks onto the streets* of New York *where they are seen and remembered* is all part of the enterprising strategy of . . . Moishe's Moving & Delivery Inc. Mr. Mana keeps his trucks on the street even if they're only delivering boxes, *just to ensure the company's name is visible.*"[1]

Trucks are rolling billboards. A 3M-financed study for the American Trucking Association Foundation of Alexandria, Virginia, shows that the "average" combination vehicle, traveling approximately 49,125 miles during the course of the year, will be seen by as many as 16 million people—94 percent of them in other moving vehicles. The cost of painting or "decalizing" such a vehicle would

---

[1] Moishe Mana, "Fast Moving Moishe's Shakes Up City's Haulers," *Crain's New York Business,* April 27, 1987.

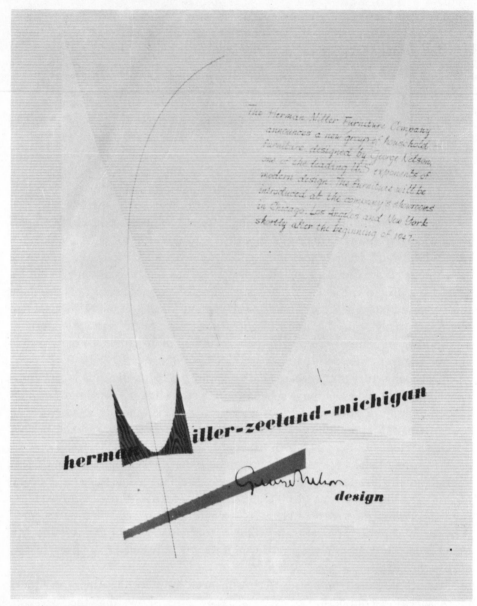

10.3 *Herman Miller*

Since the 1940's, the Herman Miller furniture company has been able to sustain design excellence. Irving Harper designed the Miller symbol in 1946 (when in George Nelson's office). The corporate identity became the consistent focal point for all communications, from the earliest ads to the latest vehicles.

Consistent use of its identity in every medium has helped Herman Miller become known as the leader in its field.

10.4 ATA reports that 16.3 million people will see a particular truck on the highways each year. Paid and unpaid advertising can work together. (1985 figures from the American Trucking Association.)

Advertisement Credit: George Nelson Associates

be in the neighborhood of $1,500, or 1/20th of what ATA says would be the cost of a "comparable" ad.

Any comparisons with stationary outdoor advertising billboards would be meaningless since no data exist on any one "printed bulletin board" (to use the Institute of Outdoor Advertising definition) that is seen over a year by 16 million people.

Yet, to indulge ATA's apples-and-oranges argument: according to the Institute of Outdoor Advertising, the *least* one could pay in car-bound Los Angeles for one of those famous Sunset Strip outdoor billboards would be a monthly $3,250, based on 1.6 million "viewer impressions." That means one would have to buy ten boards to do what one truck can do.

Moreover, ATA points out, unlike an outdoor ad, truck signage is a one-time expense requiring little or no upkeep. "To keep impressions clear with us," says an association spokesman, "all you need is a pail of sudsy water and a garden hose."

Nonetheless, outdoor billboards can help promote the corporate image and/ or product (Figures 10.5, 10.6) and they don't only have to be billboards *per se.* Sun Oil Co. and Eastern Gas & Fuel use their corporate identity on storage tanks to great advantage, and an even more dramatic use of outdoors is the giant electric CITGO sign that looms over Boston's busy Kenmore Square (Figure 10.7). The latter has assumed landmark status. During the OPEC "energy crisis" in the 1970s, thinking it would be good PR to dismantle the sign, Cities Service Co. management was greeted by such a public uproar that it hastily retreated and left the sign up "in perpetuity."

Even for those companies whose symbol has not yet become that familiar, outdoor advertising may be one of the most underrated tools of the trade. Perception Research Services Inc. trackers point out that three-fourths of respondents who see a billboard "are likely to be drawn directly to their advertiser's name," whereas only one-third would spot the name in a magazine ad. And when placed near highway exit signs, recognition rises "because at this juncture the driver is most alert."

Signs, truck ads and billboards, in order to be effective, should be professionally designed and relate to other "viewer impressions" (à la corporate identity) to strengthen and relate to overall visual image.

10.5 *Great Country Bank*
Miniature replicas of their billboards were utilized at each bank teller's window to announce a name change when the Savings Bank of Ansonia became Great Country Bank.
Design Credit: Selame Design

10.6 *Kodak Billboard*
Kodak creates a three-dimensional scene in this attention-getting billboard that cleverly demonstrates the vividness of its color film while highlighting the product.

Agency: Rumrill-Hoyt Inc. Rochester, N.Y., Photographer: Clint Clemens, Billboard: Gannett Outdoor

Determining the visual marketing position for a company is an executive responsibility. Too many corporations leave sign design up to a local sign company, the interior to various fixture houses, the design of circulars, promotional signage, and window display signs to the local printer, their advertising to an agency, and the building design to a local contractor. As the corporation multiplies and grows, the chaotic and visually poor design elements dot the landscape and become the corporate image by default, not by plan. A successful identity system visually positions a company in a clear, cohesive, and consistent manner (Figures 10.8, 10.9, 10.10).

Although many of the larger franchisers maintain real estate departments, few of them are staffed with full-time architects or designers, and fewer still pay much attention to what their jumbled appearances are saying about management's self-image.

It sometimes seems as if all these roadside operators agreed that what was working for Kemmons Wilson should also work for them. For many years, at least until the environmentalists marshalled their disparate strengths and made themselves heard, it did.

10.7 *Citgo*

In the 1960's, Cities Service Company became Citgo Petroleum Company with a contemporary symbol to go with the name change. One of their advertising applications was a spectacular neon sign display in Kenmore Square, Boston, Massachusetts. The company probably didn't realize the power of its sign until 1978, when then Governor Ed King requested the company voluntarily shut off the sign as a symbolic gesture to the energy crisis. However, in 1982, when crews were dispatched to tear the sign down, a public groundswell of supporters kept it there and lit it up.

A 1983 report of the Landmark Commission concluded that the Citgo sign did fulfill the criteria definition of a landmark, i.e., "in whole or part, (the Citgo sign) has historical, social, cultural, architectural, or aesthetic significance to the city, the commonwealth, the New England region, and the nation."

At the hearing, past president of the Society for Commercial Archeology, Luther Krim, addressed the report with this testimony, "The sign is the finest piece of spectacular neon advertising . . . " Citgo spent $300,000 to restore and maintain the sign's former version of grandeur, a great image maker.

Design Credit: Lippincott & Margulies, Inc.

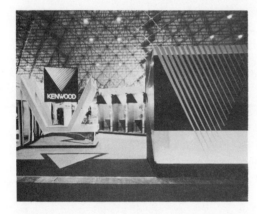

10.8, 10.9, 10.10 *Kenwood*
Global Marketing Strategy
A good mark can help to enhance any environment when tastefully applied. The Kenwood triangle and signature make a universally sharp, crisp statement in architectural signing, exhibits, advertising, equipment and packaging, translatable world-wide.

Design Credit: PAOS, Inc., Tokyo, Japan

One of the first to see that it would not work over the long haul and that, ultimately, these industries would pay a heavy price for their environmental insensitivity, was Rawleigh Warner, Jr.

In early 1965 he'd just been promoted to the presidency of Socony-Mobil Oil and one of his first actions was to persuade chairman Al Nickerson to "upgrade" the company's service station architecture.* Warner had come out of Socony-Mobil's international operations, and he felt America could learn something from Europe.

As he firmly believed in hiring the best available talent regardless of price, he retained IBM's industrial design consultant Eliot Noyes, and the two set out for a swing out west.

"It was a vast wasteland out there," he recalls. "Every gas station seemed to have streamers, those silver and gold doodads that twisted in the wind, and it got to the point where you couldn't tell ours apart from the next fellows. Ours were bad enough.

"They all seemed to be elongated, rectangular boxes covered with porcelain squares, and in the poorer parts of town our people had to post guards and install fences to keep people from stealing the squares at night. You see, they made for perfect little ashtrays."

Noyes was struck by an anomaly: the stations they visited all catered exclusively to the automobile, "yet no station used the wheel as a symbol for its trade." It inspired him to design a round gas pump, which no one had ever thought of before. And round pumps inevitably led them to think of round graphics (Figures 10.11, 10.12, 10.13, 10.14).†

At least Mobil's architectural image was *uniformly* bad. Not so Amoco's whose stations were a nightmare of bad building design: not just enameled "boxes" but service stations done up as rundown antebellum mansions, Cape Cod colonials, "pumpers" with mansard roofs, ranch houses with Doric columns—the price of uncontrolled growth.

---

*The original Vacuum Oil Company was one of the 34 units pried out of John D. Rockfeller's monopolistic Standard Oil Trust. The "Standard" name was selected in 1870 to imply quality standardization at a time the fledgling industry was run by buccaneers. Its original symbol was a gargoyle, which was replaced by the Pegasus (flying red horse) in 1931 following merger with Socony (Standard Oil Company of New York).

The merged company marketed its products under the brand name of Mobil—as in Mobilgas, Mobiloil, Mobilgard (based on the words "motion" and "mobility"). In 1955, the company became Socony-Mobil, and in 1966, 18 months after Warner was elected president, the last tie to Standard Oil was cut when the Socony name was dropped. The Pegasus symbol survives, albeit as a secondary trademark on tank cars and industrial facilities the general public seldom sees. "It's a bit of our past," says Warner. "We consider it of high importance and inestimable sentimental value."

†Round, *visible* graphics: Chermayeff & Geismar's Ivan Chermayeff recognized that gas station signage would have to be readable at 65 mph from at least half a mile down the road, "otherwise the motorist would not have time to slow down and exit."

"The only thing consistent about our identity back in 1979," remembers Abdul Azhari, Amoco market research director, "was its inconsistency."[2]

Given Amoco's size—4,000 owned service stations, as many as 8,000 independent or "jobber" stations—one can imagine just how widespread the inconsistency was at the time the company took stock of itself, what it represented, and where it hoped to be going.

"Before we undertook our redesign program," says Azhari, "our stations projected an uncared-for image. Our stations were of different generations of architecture and signage and many looked run-down and old."[3]

"If you *look* like you don't care, you begin to *act* like you don't care, and then you develop the *reputation* of not caring,"[4] says Azhari.

But before things got to that dismal point, Amoco surveyed more than 50,000 motorists, ostensibly to determine what people expected of their neighborhood gas station. The survey, part of what management referred to as "The Image Project," confirmed public awareness of the physical deterioration and signage chaos.

Yet it revealed a rock-solid customer loyalty to Amoco brands. No one had trouble recalling its torch and oval symbol. So, before one feeling could overpower the other, the company committed itself to a sequential but comprehensive program of modernizing its stations and adding new consumer services and products that would allow Amoco to stay competitive.

"We weren't just talking about simply cleaning up stations and painting a few rusty spots and removing the oil patches, but making dramatic changes in both style and substance," recalls Azhari.

But not too dramatic. Under the New Environmentalism, the sleekest rehab may turn out to be as unwelcome as the dump it replaced. Long after Mobil had implemented its ultramodern Noyes stations, recalls Rawleigh Warner, "We would run smack into local building codes." For example, in the tiny Los Angeles suburb of Pacific Palisades, former home of President Ronald Reagan, "We had to come up with a kind of adobe-style service station that would blend into the local environment. If we'd said to them, 'Sorry, we only have one design and that's it,' they'd have kept us out for good."[5]

As other oil companies have found, a new look often leads to other service innovations. In Amoco's case, it was the Certicare auto repair program that set their full-service units apart from competing "backyard" mechanics and body shops. Certicare, treated as a separate "product," was given its own theme-related design treatment (Figures 10.15, 10.16, 10.17).

---

[2]Personal interview of Abdul Azhari by authors.
[3]*Ibid.*
[4]*Ibid.*
[5]Personal interview of Rawleigh Warner Jr. by author.

10.11

10.12

10.11–10.14 *Mobil*
Design Credits, Architectural: Elliot Noyes; Corporate Identity: Chermayeff & Geismar

10.13

10.14

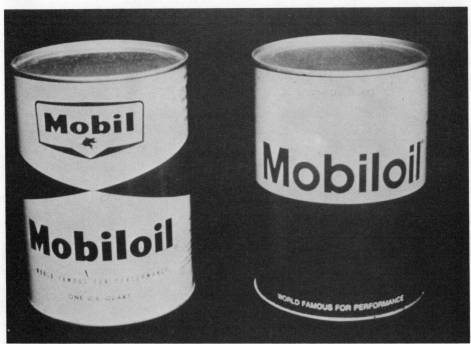

Anticipating that further change awaits gas marketers by the end of this century, Amoco placed particular emphasis on self-service, then just getting under way. Much attention was paid to making signage far more self-explanatory and to lighting—responding to consumer concern over security in a self-service environment. More than 50 percent of Amoco's customers are women.

In many redesigned sites, business increased by as much as 300 percent, and over a period of five years, the corporate image of Amoco rose even more dramatically.

Not content to rest on its laurels,* Amoco's experimental prototype of its Station of the Future is actively being researched and developed. The first test station is already up in Kansas, the land of Oz. The second opened appropriately in Orlando, the land of Epcot, and will be followed by a selective rollout (Figures 10.18, 10.19, 10.20).

The increasing level of environmental awareness that is bringing a refreshing new look to the corner service station is now beginning to transform another roadside industry—the convenience food store. It's a logical progression, since many C-stores either were or still are integral parts of the oil industry. In a relatively few years, C-stores have become a $200 billion industry that could, in time, offer serious competition to the nation's smaller supermarkets (of which more will be discussed in the next chapter).

Leading the way in this image upscaling, as it should, is the industry's progenitor, Dallas' Southland Corporation. Southland intends to give the C-store an entirely different identity.

Instead of continuing to serve the public as an "emergency stop," it wants C-stores to operate as "destination" stops—in short, to go toe-to-toe with the neighborhood supermarket at a time the supermarket is undergoing a wrenching identity change.

Back in 1957, the Southland Ice Company of Dallas had a better idea: since most of its regular business took place either very early in the morning or very late at night, when most groceries were closed, it would accommodate its customers by also selling them cigarettes, candies, snacks, even such staples as milk and bread, off the same loading dock where they picked up their blocks and bags of ice.

With suburbia on the rise, Southland next built a network of small mom & pop-type stores—but *without* mom or pop—that would sell "emergency grocery supplies" well into the evening hours. They were referred to as "seven-elevens" after the 7 a.m. to 11 p.m. hours) and the name took hold. By 1968, Southland Corp., no longer just an ice maker, was reporting over $1 billion sales at its 7–Elevens.

---

*The concept and execution of the Amoco Station of the Future program, as developed by Selame Design, received the 1988 Industrial Design Excellence Award from the Industrial Designers Society of America because accroding to the IDEA jurors, "it stood out above all others. . . (and) made a significant contribution to the reputation of US design."
Charles W. Pelly, IDSA
1988 IDEA Jury Chair

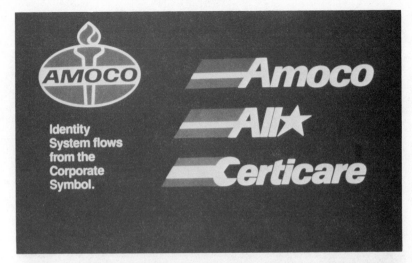

10.15

10.16

10.17

10.15–10.20 *Amoco*
Design Credit: Selame Design

10.18

10.19

10.20

10.18, 10.19, 10.20

Others jumped in, such as Circle-K (now the industry's second biggest chain after 7-Eleven's 8,200 units) Stop 'n Go, Dairy Mart, and its newly acquired Lawson's, Cumberland Farms, Store 24, Quick-Chek, etc. (Figures 10.20, 10.21).

Parking lots were added. It also made sense to add an off-brand gas pump or two for patrons low on gas. It was a cash-only business to tide drivers over until they could make a credit-card buy the next day.

The move did not escape the attention of the major oil companies. In the 1970s, Detroit's extended maintenance warranties were emptying their service bays, idling mechanics; OPEC's two oil embargoes were driving up gas prices, causing a sharp drop in business. The majors began shrinking their service station empires, but found few takers for the moribund real estate.

To keep surviving dealer organizations viable, an additional income stream had to be found. The C-store concept seemed tailor-made; after all, most gas stations had been selling snacks to motorists along with maps and windshield wipers. As the demand for tires, batteries, and automobile parts shrank, the hunger for sandwiches and coffee grew.

Today, about 40 percent of the nation's 65,000 C-stores are owned and operated by or affiliated with oil companies. Some oil companies are even now talking about converting some of their large C-stores into full-fledged roadside restaurants for motorists in search of a total fill-up.

The image problems of America's roadside merchants become even more convoluted as more of them reverse gears and strike out for new locations in the heart of the cities.

McDonald's Golden Arches, which came into being in the 1950s as an inspired Ray Kroc gimmick to make the small red and white-tiled roadside stands look bigger than they actually were, are obviously inappropriate on the cityscape.

In New York City, the very idea of having "roadside stand" architecture integrated into high-rise buildings sent local community planning boards scurrying to the statute books, after which they set out to galvanize community opposition on a grand scale.

In 1974, McDonald's sought a location in Manhattan's "Silk Stocking" district—66th Street and Lexington Avenue. There was a "tremendous uprising," recalls Howard J. Rubenstein, whose high-powered, politically connected PR firm was brought in to try to win over the community. It made no difference how many teenagers they pledged to put to work. McDonald's was denied a building license.

Undeterred, but now much more sensitive to the aesthetic needs of New Yorkers, McDonald's found other locations where it could fit right in without having to turn the places into sidewalk eyesores. "The 66th Street episode was a turning point for the company," says Rubenstein. "They learn fast out there in Oak Brook."

10.20, 10.21 *Store 24*
A Visual Connection
Store 24's identity is followed through in departmental identification. By using one typestyle and color scheme, secondary names become "part of the family" when used for departments, services, and private label products.

Design Credit: Selame Design

They have to, especially if they want to continue their overseas expansion. In many old world countries, the restrictive building codes are far tougher than they are here, and officials are far less tolerant of U.S. companies imposing their mass-market blueprints on local economies that value indigenous architecture.

There now is growing recognition that unless the interface environment — external as well as internal—is pleasing to the eye, all of the monies being expended on such point-of-purchase aesthetics as brand naming, symbolism, and packaging may be wasted. And after a slow start, this recognition is also taking hold in the public and institutional sectors of healthcare, higher education, federal, state, and local government—especially in the areas of public transportation.

In the early 1960s, the Commonwealth of Massachusetts, seeking to reduce automobile congestion in downtown Boston, enacted special tax legislation on cigarettes that would help defray a $400 million rehabilitation and expansion program bringing mass transit to 78 outlying cities and towns. At least $20 million of this went to upgrade environmental architecture, directional signage, and route mapping for Boston's squeaky old subway system. Peter Chermayeff, partner in the master planning design firm of Cambridge Seven Associates, explains, "What's the use of modernizing anything if people don't know their way around the system and can't use it?"

A question similar to Chermayeff's was posed by President Richard M. Nixon shortly after settling into his first term. He had in mind a bigger system than mass transit: the federal government itself.

An admitted Anglophile, Nixon had admired the British program of encouraging greater public awareness of industrial and graphic design. Various private and state visits to Canada left him with a favorable impression of that country's graphic unification program. Could something similar take hold here?

He knew he could never get Congressional budget approval to set up the equivalent of the British Design Council, which had influenced the Canadian government. BDC, funded by H.R.M. Department of Industry, supplements its budget by selling its consulting services to the private sector.

But Congress, in effect, had already established the machinery for such an operation when it created the National Endowment for the Arts; and its head, the charismatic Nancy Hanks, enjoyed an excellent rapport with the powerful committee chairmen on the Hill. A good place to start, she told the White House, would be to launch a Federal Graphics Improvement Program that for the first time in the Republic's history would give all federal communications—signs, publications, forms, letterheads, etc.—a cohesive, unified appearance. To create a set of standards, Nixon—through Hanks—convened the first Federal Design Assembly in April 1973.

It brought to Washington the nation's visual design establishment—some of the top names from all the various graphics disciplines—and produced a sort of

Ten Commandments, some of whose tenets are applicable to the private sector and bear repeating here. As the Assembly agreed, visual design:

- *promotes greater identification* among employees and the general public of organizations and their missions;
- *encourages standards of clarity, appropriateness,* and *uniformity* in all communications;
- *saves time and money* through more efficient use of materials and their production.

Knowing the bureaucracy's penchant for going only half the distance, the Assembly also agreed that "improvements" made with little forethought, or real purpose, invariably produce piecemeal "solutions" which rather quickly turn out to be no solutions at all, merely new problems.

Ironically, this was precisely what happened to the Federal Graphics Improvement Program. Intensified through the prism of petty politics, the well-intentioned Hanks plan, at first applauded, soon was perceived as a threat by the entrenched bureaucracy, and watered down. Entrenched bureaucrats traditionally resist any sort of change with the rubric, " . . . but that's the way we've always done things around here."

Consequently, only a handful of agencies ended up systematizing their internal and external communications—among them the CIA, NASA, Environmental Protection Administration, U.S. Army Corps of Engineers, GSA, and the Departments of Transportation, Labor, Health & Human Services.

By this time suffering terminal cancer, Mrs. Hanks could not keep up the good fight. And for all its initial encouragement, the White House—by now caught up in the Watergate quagmire—had more important fish to fry.

The moral is, according to Bill Lacy, Mrs. Hank's former deputy and now President of New York's Cooper Union for the Advancement of Science & Art, which graduates tomorrow's design leaders: "You can have all sorts of powerful connections, but never underestimate the power of the *status quo*."

'OH' AS IN MOBIL

Why is the "O" in Mobil red? Or in black-and-white ads, an open letter or two concentric circles?

"It's to help people put the correct emphasis on the first syllable," says retired Mobil chairman Rawleigh Warner Jr. "You don't say 'Moh-beel' as in Alabama."

He adds, "The red O is one of the more valuable components of the design system. Mobil is careful not to play games with it. The circular O also echoes Eliot's gas station canopy and pump design."

The only place in the world it doesn't appear is in Saudi Arabia and Egypt, but design continuity is maintained in other ways. The ubiquitous Mobil logo is seen on thousands of service stations, oil refineries, storage facilities, ocean-going tankers, highway trucks, and countless roadside signs and advertising billboards.

It is also seen as a black-and-white signature on those feisty Op-Ed page, pro-business, anti-media "advertorials" that Mobil runs in many influential newspapers, and on PBS - jocularly known as the "Petroleum Broadcasting Service"—where Mobil since 1971 has been underwriting *Masterpiece Theatre* and other highbrow fare.

It did *not* appear anywhere in or near Montgomery Wards, which Mobil owned since 1974 and sold in 1987 to Robert Brennan, the brother of Sears' CEO, in a leveraged buyout, nor is it ever used by any of Mobil's sundry non-oil subsidiaries. Until mid-1986, Mobil also owned Container Corporation of America, the world's largest manufacturer of artfully designed paperboard containers (acquired as part of the Montgomery Ward deal). It was CCA founder Walter Paepcke, one of the earliest champions of corporate identity, who started the world-renowned Aspen Design Conference in 1950.

11

Identity and the retail environment within

For San Francisco sportswear designer-retailer, Doug Tompkins, the most important letter in the alphabet is E—triple-barred, as in *Esprit.* It is not so much a letter as a symbol for one man's zeal in trying to control his retail environment—and succeeding.

"Esprit," says *Industrial Design* magazine, "uses store design consistently, strategically, and evangelistically."

Esprit began in 1970 as just another California sportswear label going after the 18-to-34-year-old market. Over the next 17 years, it grew to become one of the hottest new lines in more than 2,100 retail and department stores (down from 4,000 a few years ago). Tompkin's merchandising ideas were so advanced, his display design criteria so high and exacting, his beliefs so intense, and the response of some stores so sluggish, that Tompkins cut back on host department stores and began building his own, where he would be the undisputed master of his own retail environment from A to Z.

Few manufacturers are willing or able to do this. Many would like to, but are chary of tilting with store management. Vendors seldom win turf wars in host stores.

Esprit apparently has enough clout to force host store managers to grit their teeth and look the other way as Tompkins' army of industrial designers under the appropriately named Aura Oslapas literally rebuild that part of the stores that will house the Esprit collection. New walls are erected, lighting fixtures hung, dressing rooms and counters installed. Esprit uses its own hardware, custom-designed not to dominate the clothes (as the hardware of many other stores are likely to do).

What sets Esprit apart from most other high-fashion specialty manufacturers-cum-retailers is not cause but effect: its identity is never in doubt. All the various small mosaics that make up Esprit's visual image seem to flow together seamlessly (Figures 11.1, 11.2).

Tompkins recognized that as retailer as well as designer, Esprit is at once part of two, often conflicting, soft goods industries—one that makes trends, the other that follows them. By insisting on controlling its own display areas, Esprit says it is unwilling to put its fate in the hands of others.

Retail identity

Tompkins is of a new breed that recognizes that when it comes to protecting image and identity, the changing rules of the retail game have a lot of players sitting between the proverbial rock and a hard place.

The old rules no longer work, now that it's hard to tell where the manufac-

11.1, 11.2 *Esprit*
Design Credit: John Casado

turer ends and the retailer begins, or when a pharmacy stops being a pharmacy and becomes a mass merchandiser.

Identity and image, always important in retailing for over 3,000 years, become even more so when giant corporations start slugging it out in Main Street store fronts: most Federal Express street-level "shops" are so immaculately groomed that it seems odd to realize that they are nothing but drop-off points for overnight packages. The U.S. Postal Service makes no such efforts, but then the "post office" runs a monopoly.

Store environment has always mattered, but never so much as when store identities are becoming more fragile in the face of unanticipated competition.

What is one to make of this scene? On a rainy Tuesday in April an unlicensed Senegalese sidewalk merchant, setting up "shop" not ten feet from the front doors of Lord & Taylor, is doing a landslide business selling fake Lord & Taylor umbrellas!

Everyone, it seems, is targeting the same shopper, traveling essentially the same road, and it is a wonder so few collide. "Who needs stores," asks a $120,000-a-year Wall Street broker, "when I can get merchandise as good as or better by mail from Lands' End?"

There are some who say the days of the traditional granite-faced, block-long department store are numbered, beset on one flank by the shopping mall, on the other by Esprit-like specialty stores. Even those less pessimistic about the future of the department store say that the ones that will survive will be unrecognizable, looking more and more like collections of specialty stores.

Kurt Barnard, publisher of *Barnard's Retail Marketing Report*, says that in many of the Bloomingdale's mall stores, "as you walk down the corridor you suddenly find yourself surrounded by shops on the left and right, and you think you are still inside the mall, but actually you're inside Bloomdingdale's."[1]

Bloomie's is one of the giants that seems to have made a successful accommodation with the dreaded enemy, the specialty store. Barnard thinks that given the current rate of growth—six times that of the department stores—the apparel chain industry by the 1990s will top $50 billion.

For department store retailers, the challenge is clear: to find and keep a niche identity that will either allow them to co-exist profitably on their terms, or to upgrade their total store environments to better compete with the upstarts.

Those that haven't are paying a steep price. They are either folding, are being downsized and sold off piecemeal as have the various marginal units of the Allied Stores Corp., or, as have New York's Ohrbach's and Gimbels, are closing only to be acquired by smarter merchandisers principally for their real estate assets.

"If you're a department store and you don't make yourself beautiful and

---

[1]Personal interview of Kurt Barnard by author.

appealing to that very affluent women who wants to buy designer apparel," says store consultant Howard Davidowitz, "forget it."[2]

To most department store merchandisers, hugeness can be both a plus and a minus. "If you're running a 4,000 square foot specialty store," says Davidowitz, "you can't do what a 200,000 square foot store can do. A store designer can make a presentation of handbags 15 times the size of any specialty store. Go to Macy's and look at the accessories department. My God, it's enormous."[3]

But Kurt Barnard takes the opposite tack. "Today's shopper doesn't have time to roam around on endless floors, to fight their way onto elevators, to wade through aisles of things that don't interest them and look for sales help that isn't there."

In contrast, specialty stores sell convenience. "They zero in on their customers and quickly identify themselves in window displays. The window tells you right away whether it's the kind of store that it might pay for them to walk into."[4]

In either case, it is clear that in today's rapidly changing retailing climate, store image is crucial, and as Davidowitz says, the big stores "are more beautiful than ever before, are spending a lot of money on design."[5] They've got to in order to survive the onslaught of the environmentally hip specialty retailers to whom video displays are where the future's at.

Retailing as theatre is as old as the profession itself. Only now, store ambience is becoming as important (if not more so) as the merchandise on display. One reason is sameness: one study conducted in Los Angeles shows that as much as 70 percent of the goods sold in Bullock's, Robinson's, and the May Company are "virtually identical." Private labeling may only be a partial solution.

That *changing the environment* can make a huge difference in both the fortunes and outlook of today's department store merchandisers can be seen by visiting Barney's New York on unfashionable lower Seventh Avenue. Long before that unfortunate demographic term even entered the English vernacular, the owners spent many years and many more millions of dollars shedding the store's tired, old, middle-class identity because they had correctly foreseen the inexorable rise of the Yuppie Class. Barney's is not so much a soft goods department store as a vertical mall of upscale men and women's specialty shops.

In the mid-1980s, clothing designer Ralph Lauren spent nearly $10 million to retrofit the venerable (1898) Gertrude Rhinelander Walso mansion on Manhattan's upper Madison Avenue, restoring the *fin de siècle* Victorian elegance and turning the entire structure into one vast "private club" for an upscale public.

---

[2]Howard Davidowitz, *New York Times*, 1986.
[3]Davidowitz, *ibid.*
[4]Barnard, *op. cit.*
[5]Davidowitz, *op. cit.*

It sells only one brand of clothing: *Polo*—at prices higher than the same merchandise is ticketed for at Bloomingdale's. As retail theatre, the Polo/Ralph Lauren Store is S.R.O.

Barney's and Bloomingdale's understand what it is that they have to do to attract and hold today's easily distracted, often disloyal, and much competed for "niche shoppers":

- Make the store easy to shop in with clear informational and directional signage and comfortable lighting levels. Save busy shoppers time, not just money; time *is* money.

- Make customers feel better about themselves by helping them escape from the mundane real world: make the store a stage and give them fantasy, bread and circuses.

- Make the store "user friendly" by turning it into an information center for useful, practical ideas that will brighten and elevate shoppers' lives.

- Make customers believe that only here can they depend on full service and guaranteed as well as perceived value. Pizzazz pays.

Interestingly, all these aims can be achieved strategically, through visual marketing techniques. Interior signage is only one of them, and not necessarily the most visible one. Store shopping bags are. Packaging is also a time-tested and proven technique for building and enhancing store identity: there is no mistaking the blue Tiffany's box or Bloomie's Brown Bag.

It doesn't necessarily have to cost so much money that only the big stores benefit. Integrated visual identity is as important to the small retailers as it is to the biggest ones, perhaps more so, as it can make the smaller ones look bigger than they really are.

Insuring his company's future through identity

One night in 1984, Jeffrey Ross, president of the 20-plus unit Thayer Pharmacies chain, was driving around the greater Boston area. In the course of one hour, he stopped by three of his stores, each of which was identified by a different illuminated sign. The following day, he came to see us; we'd been talking on and off for more than a year about a corporate identity program for the family-owned company that had been founded by Jeff's father in Braintree, Massachusetts, in 1939. Until that night it just didn't seem all that important to make the commitment.

Samuel Ross had named his drugstore after a local hero, Army General Sylvanus Thayer (1785–1872), the founder of the U.S. Military Academy at West Point. But when it came time to trademark the name, Ross was chagrined to learn he couldn't, not as long as there was a consumer demand for a throat lozenge named *Thayer's Slippery Elm.* Sam's response was to order some for his drugstore.

As new stores were added, exterior signage was ordered from various local signmakers, none of whom bothered to see if theirs resembled the Thayer sign in the next town.

Private label products—as many as 300—were packed for Thayer by an assortment of suppliers, each of whom had their own design formula that happened to accommodate the Thayer name and its cookie-cutter "symbol," a pharmacist's mortar and pestle. The Ross family gave visual identity scant thought; they were too busy filling prescriptions and other customer needs.

Perhaps also too busy to notice that among the new arrivals in the neighborhood, along with young growing families, were the discount druggists—the nononsense, no-service, self-service pharmacies of the future. Some were local, most were units of regional and national chains. What they lacked in personal services, they more than made up for in appearances. They looked modern, whereas — Ross realized when he got home that night—Thayer didn't.

Within twelve weeks, Thayer Pharmacies got its new corporate symbol (a wordmark) — its name in white against a blue background with a capsule-like red cross filling in the letter "a". The symbol is now considered the focal identity point that serves as a unifying graphic device on packaging, signage, uniforms, letterheads, delivery vans, etc. It opened up a world of possibilities—and applications. Thayer made the most of them. The entire private label line was repackaged—with the Thayer name and mark appearing even on the tiniest Rx capsule. From packaging, the identity system was extended to store interiors.

The one thing we did not touch was the way Thayer conducts its business. It was fine just as it was. In terms of providing personalized attention, nothing has changed. "We are still warm and friendly," says Jeffrey Ross, "although to the big guys down the street, I'm sure we don't look it anymore."[6] Although Thayer is still a small fish in a small pond, as it was when we were asked in, now it swims a great deal more confidently (Figures 11.3, 11.4, 11.5, 11.6, 11.7, 11.8).

Change for the sake of change seems to be endemic in mass-market retailing, irrespective of what business they're in. Modern merchandising cannot operate well or long in a static environment. Yet, for some retailers desirous of developing and maintaining identities uniquely their own, too much change too often turns out to be destructive—and not always in the long run. Why should that be?

One reason may be that while shoppers say they welcome change, most turn

---

[6]Personal interview of Jeffrey Ross by author.

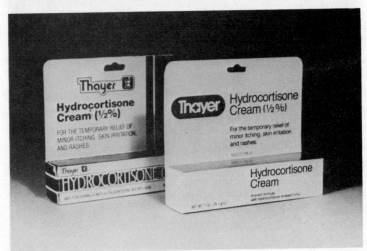

11.3–11.8 *Thayer*

Design Credit: Selame Design

out to be creatures of habit. They enjoy shopping in familiar surroundings; they intensely dislike having to "re-learn" the physical layout of a store that has undergone structural change. As the old pun goes, familiarity breeds content.

Thus, revamping store layouts should be undertaken only *if* and *when* there's good reason to do so. The visual improvements should be just that — improvements. One way of determining whether anticipated physical changes will, indeed, impact favorably on earnings, is to follow the example of J.C. Penney.

Before Penney's embarked on its massive image upgrading program, it spent a lot of time getting to know its customers, how they had changed, and how Penney's hadn't.

Former J.C. Penney product design manager Cooper Woodring says, "One of the things we learned was that Americans no longer shopped categorically, you know, looking for products by what they could afford—'good' quality, or 'best.'"

Stores were laid out to emphasize the "better" grades, since retailers instinctively knew, says Woodring, "that 'better' sold 'best.'"

Now, in the affluent 1970s and 1980s, shoppers no longer looked for "better" but could afford "best." But the department stores were generally slow to catch on. Their store layouts changed very little. They didn't see the floor as supermarketers see theirs: as strategic battlefields.

"We finally figured it out," say Woodring. "Today's better-educated consumer makes two kinds of purchases, call them 'sacrificial' and 'enhanced.'"

"They'll buy the family clothes at discount, the food at warehouse prices, feed the kids at McDonald's, but they'll be driving a new Mercedes SL-600. To make that one 'enhancement' purchase, people make all sorts of 'sacrificial' buys."

Penney's decided it didn't only want to sell "sacrificially." It went upscale—but not to Bloomingdale's extent (Figures 11.9, 11.10).

Interestingly, Bloomie's hired as its design consultant Massimo Vignelli, who had been one of the principals at Unimark during its tenure with Penney's. He gave it a visual identity that, says Bloomingdale's president, Marvin Traub, "changed our character, our product mix, our customer demographics. Our slogan, 'like no other store in the world,' is no longer just a slogan. It's an indisputable fact."[7]*

Bloomingdale's management will not say what it cost. Few department stores are willing to share such information. "I don't think the public really wants to

---

*An apocryphal story making the rounds of New York's retailing circles has it that when the publisher of the city's leading, but sleazy, tabloid newspaper boasted of his circulation gains to Traub by way of trying to get Bloomie's to advertise, he was told, "My friend, you don't seem to understand. Your *readers* are our *shoplifters.*"

[7] Personal interview of Marvin Traub by author.

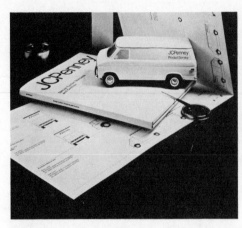

11.9, 11.10 *J. C. Penney*
Design Credit: Massimo Vignelli and J. C. Penney Design Department

know," says an executive of Washington's Woodward & Lothrop, which underwent a major rehabilitation in 1986.

Times change. It wasn't that long ago that the quickest way to give a store's treasurer apoplexy was to suggest a modernization of the premises. Cooper Woodring recalls that during Penney's corporate identity change, "stores that had been modernized at a cost of $5 million each had to be redone after the fourth year." What caused Penney's bean counters such anguish was that such massive store outlays could be amortized over the next 20 years.

Woodring says, "Where they ever got that idea, God knows. Accountants do not understand that retailers are like car dealers: they only sell what's currently in style."[8]

Mall identity: yours, mine, or ours?

That styles change from minute to minute can be seen most clearly on the vastly larger canvas of today's shopping center. For it is here that all the elements of environmental design come together in myriad ways on a magnified scale.

It used to be an article of faith among real estate developers that, in life, only three things really mattered: location, location, and location. Now it's four: *identity*.

Every shopping center or mall developer wants his property to be seen, recognized, and remembered. To do this, each must make the firm commitment to visual identity even before the ground-breaking ceremony takes place. The name and symbol given the development thus becomes as critical a factor as the site itself. Name and symbol often reflect the ideal tenant mix the developer seeks, and can play as important a role in attracting prospective tenants as it will drawing store traffic later on (Figure 11.11).

Shopping centers are never truly "finished," but keep on growing—making it even more crucial that the visual identity is both flexible and adaptable without becoming a visual cliché. The older the shopping center, the more important the visuals—as they can keep such retail environments looking young (Figure 11.12).

What the developer must always keep in mind, however, is that as important as the development's visual identity may be—and no matter how ambitious and widespread its implementation—it cannot afford to ignore the visual presentation and identities of the project's tenants.

For any retail operation to prosper in these days of growing consumer affluence, it must not only enjoy a clearly defined market position and steady repeat patronage by a loyal customer base, but must stock a product mix either priced or styled to suit.

It must also make shopping a pleasurable experience, for if not, the war is lost by default to the mail order merchants who will be happy to fill virtually every imaginable consumer need.

---

[8]Personal interview of Cooper Woodring by author.

11.11 *Oakwell Farms*
A unique sign for a San Antonio shopping center says it all, without words.
Design Credit: Bradford Lawton Design

These days, with leases costing more and running longer, no merchant can afford to do what his father might have done just 15 years ago: close early and hope for a better day tomorrow.

An attractive, well-kept store tells customers that management appreciates their values, values their patronage, and is willing to treat them as guests. And by letting those customers know from the *outside* what they can expect to find *inside,* and make finding the item in demand easy, management also tells the customers "we want what you want."

Retail managers should also tell it to the property owner. All upscale developers want their projects—building, shopping center, enclosed mall—to have an upscale image, and they are prepared to go to great lengths to secure such upscale "anchor" tenants as Saks Fifth Avenue, Woodward & Lothrop's, Marshall Field's, Neiman-Marcus, I. Magnin, or Bullock's. Once these are in hand, they will start to orchestrate their developments so as to create a certain kind of traffic flow around the anchors—Ann Taylor, Brookstone, Banana Republic, Crate & Barrel, Williams-Sonoma, Laura Ashley, Barnes & Noble, etc.

They need these not so much for prestige—although this should not be discounted—as for the money. An executive at the Hahn Company of San Diego, developer of prestigious Horton Plaza and other prize-winning shopping complexes, explains: "We look for tenants who do tremendous grosses, say over $600 a year *per square foot,* because their leases are structured on percentages of store

11.12 *Paramus Park*
Paramus Mall identifies its entrance with a unifying symbol, both free standing and over the mall's entrance. The mark is also carried through interior directionals and promotional materials.

Design: The Rouse Company

sales." So developers will invest in building the stage but expect the tenants to create imaginative stage sets.* This is especially critical in the fast-growing category of "festival centers" such as Rouse's Quincy Markets in downtown Boston and Harborside in Baltimore, or out west, in San Francisco's Ghirardelli Square and The Cannery.

---

*A new study by the International Council of Shopping Centers shows average operating expenses for enclosed malls to run about $2.86 per square foot of the total gross leasable space, of which 70 cents goes to maintenance and repair, 36 cents for marketing, 29 cents for utilities, the remainder for security, insurance, taxes, and administration.

"The storefront has become the retailer's image, and if it hasn't, it should" says a New York City broker representing a number of European retail chains now expanding in the U.S. "We assume shoppers don't actually ever *read* the name of the store. They *recognize* the store by its distinctive frontage. There's no mistaking a Laura Ashley from far away—the green door, the distinctive oval logo painted on the show window. Why else would Polo spend as much as $175 a square foot to acheive its polished brass and wood uniformity?"

Once inside the door, anything goes. Interior display is even more critical to store success than exterior frontage, or even the show window display. And nothing is more important than signage. Impulse shopping requires a positive mental attitude about the store and its products; consumers are not likely to be impressed by a dazzling display if it takes a road map and clerical directions to find the right spot. They don't want to reward a store that confuses and frustrates them.

Shigeru Okada of Japan's Mitsukoshi department store, whose U.S. outpost in the Ritz Tower on Park Avenue also contains an expensive Japanese restaurant, thinks American retailers do not do enough to satisfy the psychological desires of their customers.

"The big retailers here carry similar merchandise at similar prices and promote their goods in a similar manner. This has brought them to a certain level, but where can they go now when their costs are constantly increasing?"[9]

The successful stores of the future, he asserts, will be "those that can satisfy the public's *intangible* needs. Stores must not just be places to shop but places where people can congregate and enjoy themselves."[10]

Colombe Nicholas, president of Christian Dior-New York, agrees. "Stores," she says, "really have to personalize. They have to let customers know that their store is special, and also *why* it is special."[11]

It is no accident that the impetus for upgrading store environments comes from abroad, where retailers, meticulous about display and the use of color, have long stressed store ambiance—and not just in selling wearing apparel.

- Sir Terence Conran, founder of Great Britain's Habitat home furnishings chain (officially known as Storehouse PLC) in 1978 became the prime tenant in New York's aluminum-sheathed Citicorp Center. His multilevel Conran's housewares emporium has spawned Storehouse's newest U.S. retail venture, Mothercare. Year-end 1987 will see no fewer than 75 of these specialty shops throughout the U.S. selling maternity, infants, and children's clothing as well as strollers, beds, and toys.

---

[9]Shigeru Okada, *New York Times*, 1986.
[10]Okada, *ibid.*
[11]Colombe Nicholas, *New York Times*, 1986.

- Laura Ashley Holdings PLC came into the U.S. market two years before Conran, initially in San Francisco, then on that stretch of upper Madison Avenue called "Rodeo Drive East." It has since added 105 units, intends to go to 200, mainly in upscale urban markets. Currently Ashley operates over 250 stores in thirty countries.
- Aca Joe, a recent arrival in men's casual sportswear, was founded in 1975 in Acapulco by an expatriate American sweater designer. Now with over 100 stores, it is going after the same yuppie market as Benetton.

The latter, famous for cookie-cutter stores, coordinated by carefully controlled indentity, and its riotously colored Italian knitwear, is referred to by the business press as "the McDonald's of fashion." It is an apt description, as in many U.S. cities, there now seems to be at least three Benetton stores each with its Benetton sign on every block. A slight exaggeration, perhaps: it will have only 700 shops here by early 1988, but expects to go to twice that number by 1990.

Luciano Benetton, who presides over the family-run business from a 17th-century villa outside Venice, claims an annual 20 percent growth rate and net profits exceeding 10 percent—well above the industry norm. The reason he opens up so many stores so close to each other, he explains, is "each store, because of its retail identity and colorful contents, is a billboard advertisement for the next." Benetton presently has 4,000 units in sixty countries.

Super images by design

Another retail area where "European-style" store design is having a profound impact is in the food market. Here, too, all the world's a stage, and the products mere players.

The supermarket was invented in the USA, but it is taking the Europeans to show us how to make them visually appealing—and profitable.

In 1973, Sir James Goldsmith, the controversial Anglo-French head of a $2 billion conglomerate of energy, pulp and paper, publishing, and food distribution companies, bought control of the ailing Grand Union supermarkets, an east coast chain. He spent the first few years checking out most of Grand Union's 370 stores, concluding more was needed than the usual spruce-up.

He hired the raconteur Milton Glaser, pop artist, magazine designer, and gourmet cook to synthesize his two interests in the redesign of Grand Union.

Sir Jimmy's plan was to convert the stores into service-oriented gourmet centers, offering fresh-baked bread, pears poached in cassis, ready-to-cook stuffed Rock Cornish hens. He set up training courses to teach clerks the difference between Brie and Chevre. And he gave Glaser free rein.

11.13, 11.14, 11.15 *Grand Union*
Grand Union's red dot not only serves as a signal device on signs but is used promotionally in point-of-purchase posters and advertisements highlighting specials.

Design Credit: Milton Glaser

He took it. To date, Glaser's redesign of Grand Union along European lines has cost Goldsmith at least $1.5 million *per* store. Over 100 stores have been remodeled so far. In some, sales have quintupled, and Sir Jimmy attributes much of the turnaround to Glaser's environmental graphics (Figures 11.13, 11.14, 11.15).

The executive to whom Glaser reported in the beginning, Goldsmith's manager, Scottish-born James M. Wood, now works for rival A&P as CEO—having been hired away in 1980 by Tengelmann Group, at the time a $3-billion operator of 2,000 West German food stores.

He is applying to A&P much of what he learned from Milton Glaser at Grand Union, and partly as a result of this, has managed to restore the company to profitability after just two years.

Founded in 1869 by George Huntington Hartford and leather importer George Francis Gilman, The Great Atlantic & Pacific Tea Company had grown by 1934 to become the world's largest food chain, operating 15,709 stores in 34 states.*

Now down to 1,000 stores in twenty-five states, with sales over $9 billion, A&P, according to business historian Milton Moskowitz, "permanently changed American food retailing from a labor-intensive service industry with high margins to volume-oriented, low-cost, low-profit, standardized chains that insisted on uniformity and consistent standards of quality."[12]

A&P did not invent supermarketing; it was forced into it by others in the late 1930s. But once it did, A&P grew so big so fast that for many years it was a permanent target for Congressional trust-busters.

What Congress failed to do to A&P, the company's own moss-backed management did to itself. While competitors were staking out suburbia in the 1960s and early 1970s, A&P stuck to the dying inner cities, plowing profits into sustaining its antiquated food processing facilities—coffee roasters, fisheries, jam and jelly makers, milk processing plants, bakeries, condiment packers—all sources for its Ann Page store brands. At the time, shoppers were moving *away* from store brands.

In 1973, Safeway ousted A&P from the top run; A&P's Old Guard had died off, but new management failed to stanch the hemorrhaging red ink. They closed

---

*Gilman also was A&P's first store designer. According to Moskowitz, et al. [*Everybody's Business: The Irrelevant Guide to Corporate America* (New York, 1980: Harper & Row)]: "The front of the first store on Vesey Street in New York was painted with 'real vermillion imported from China,' with touches of gold leaf which reflected the light of the capital 'T' illuminated in gas over the doorway. The windows were festooned with red, white and blue globes. Inside tea bins copied the facade in bright reds and gold. The cashier's cages were built to resemble miniature Chinese pagodas. In the center of the store a large cockatoo squawked 'welcome,' and on Saturday nights a band played free."

[12]Personal interview of Milton Moskowitz by F. Peter Model.

down half of its then 3,500 stores, but the move was likened by one Wall Street analyst to "rearranging the deck chairs on the Titanic." In 1978, Kroger pushed A&P to third place. By acquiring Jewel Tea, Utah-based American Stores then pushed A&P to fourth place, where it remains today.

James Wood sees nothing demeaning in that. "Large-volume sales aren't the total answer," he insists. "High market share and good profit return on a local level are." He intends to "operate as many dominant regional chains as we can."[13]

To that end, Wood's A&P has been spending about $365 million to upgrade old-line A&Ps into "Futurestores," gobbling up the likes of Kohl's in Wisconsin, Dominion in Ontario, and in New York—where in 1987 it ousted Pathmark to become Number One with a twenty percent share of market—141 Waldbaums and 54 Shopwell markets.

Included in the latter are twenty-eight very upscale but unprofitable Food Emporiums, constructed at a cost of $5 million each. Despite their current low profitability, these full-service, 24-hour pleasure domes are seen by the food industry as prototypes of tomorrow's supermarkets, where environment counts for as much as the foods being sold.

The Food Emporiums might better be called "foodworks," since many of the fresh foods are actually made or "worked" on the premises. This fact alone, says former Emporium designer Herb Ross, "attaches a great premium to lighting. Foods have got to look appetizing and fresh," which is something the old tubular fluorescent lighting cannot do.

(Ross has been a staunch advocate of ripping out all existing lighting and replacing it with real or artificial "skylighting" ever since D'Agostino Brothers retained his firm right after the OPEC crisis to cut energy costs. "It was my epiphany. I suddenly realized that for all these years store builders had been flooding the aisles with light, causing the eyes to squint, making it harder to see the shelved products which, of course, were not properly illuminated. It opened my eyes to the possibilities.")[14]

At A&P, Wood's Glaser is industrial designer Robert Gersin, whose new black-and-white Futurestores are making excellent use of pictographs—depictions of products set in black against otherwise unadorned white walls (Figure 11.16).

This "high-tech" approach to food marketing is revolutionary in store signage and communication, at once ending shopper disorientation and reminding shoppers at every turn of any purchases they may have forgotten to make.

The black-and-white approach, Gersin explains, "serves as a counterpoint to multicolored food, food packaging, even to the customers and staff."[15] And like

---

[13]James Wood, *New York Times*, 1986.
[14]Personal interview of Herb Ross by F. Peter Model.
[15]Personal interview of Robert Gersin by author.

11.16 *A & P*
Interior signage is visible on the exterior, providing A & P a major statement area—they
use it to show the history of A & P's trademark evolution.

Design Credit: Robert Gersin

Ross, Gersin has paid particular attention to lighting to make sure there are no
shadows that might keep products on the lowest shelves literally in the dark.

So far, the new and renovated Futurestores have resulted in average market-
basket sale increases of from 25 to 100 percent.

"It's so simple once you understand it," agrees Mil Batten. "It's not myste-
rious, difficult, expensive in the realm of things. I always come back to, pardon
the expression, 'the bottom line.' Not that I am profit crazy, that's what we're in
it for. A good profit reflects in a sense the kind of service you are giving the customer. It is the best barometer we have of whether customers like what we are
doing or not.

"I say that if you are really interested in the bottom line, and corporate management certainly is, you have to pay attention to visual marketing strategy.
Where some fall off is the failure to realize that corporate, product and retail identity design systems are part of the bottom line. I think it should be high on their
priorities."[16]

---

[16]Personal interview of William (Mil) Batten by author.

Index